THE MASTER'S TOUCH

Embracing Your Unique Purpose Despite Labels

By Kenneth R. Gillard

© 2025 KRG Publishing. All rights reserved.

DEDICATION

I would like to dedicate this book to my mother, the late Mrs. Effie M. Bridges Gillard.

For your love. For your sacrifice. For loving and raising me. I would not be the man that I am today if not for your sacrifice. Thank you for your wisdom. Thank you for your smile. Thank you for your faithfulness. Thank you for your patience. And most of all, thank you for your love, your heart, and your spirit, and all that you've poured into me.

COPYRIGHT PAGE

The Master's Touch
©2024 Kenneth R. Gillard
All rights reserved.

No part of this publication may be reproduced, stored in a retrieval system, or transmitted in any form or by any means — electronic, mechanical, photocopying, recording, or otherwise — without the prior written permission of the author, except in the case of brief quotations embodied in critical articles or reviews.

This book is a work of nonfiction based on the life experiences, insights, and personal reflections of the author. While every effort has been made to ensure the accuracy of the content, the author and publisher assume no responsibility for errors or omissions. The views expressed herein are those of the author and do not necessarily reflect those of any affiliated organizations or institutions.

All inquiries regarding rights, permissions, or usage should be directed to:

Kenneth R. Gillard
℅ KRG Publising. All rights reserved.
Printed in the United States of America.
Second Edition, August 2025

ACKNOWLEDGMENTS

For over sixty years, God has placed special people in my life who have encouraged me, supported me, and believed in me even when I couldn't believe in myself. This book wouldn't exist with out the touch of each of these individuals on my life.

To my adopted family — the late Effie Gillard, my mother; the late Ella Coleman, my grandmother; the late Marcia Sanders and Lee Ross, my sisters — thank you for your constant love and teaching me the values that have guided my life.

To my Biological family: My Grandmother Sammie McEwen. My parents: the late Raymond E Skelton (Shine), Sr. and the late Margaret Skelton, and my siblings, thank you for the connection that helped me understand more fully who I am.

To the late Pastor Roy I. Greer and wife Lois Greer; and the entire Mount Olive Baptist Church family. Thanks to the men of the church who became my spiritual fathers.

I would like to acknowledge the late Mr. William Tipper, who brought me to Mrs. Gillard's foster home at the age of one and a half. This was the introduction to what would become my family.

To Mr. Larry Simpson, my 7 th grade special education teacher. In 1974 he said: "Kenny can do anything that he sets his mind to."

To Pastor Charles Dantzler, my mentor who taught me both the Word and about being filled with the Holy Spirit — thank you for seeing something in me worth investing in and for trusting me with a class at the Genesee County jail.

To Dr. Robert Bates, my therapist — thank you for helping me tear down the wall; brick by brick and for teaching me that I wasn't slow or stupid- just differently made.

To all the teachers, pastors, church members, neighbors, and friends who saw beyond my struggles to the person God created me to be — thank you for your patience and encouragement.

To the men I met in the Genesee County jail over sixteen years of ministry — thank you for teaching me about authenticity and for showing me that God can transform any life, including my own.

To the young men I've been blessed to mentor — thank you for allowing me to pour into your lives and for the ways you've "sharpened" me in return.

And to you, the reader — thank you for allowing me to share my story with you. My prayer is that you will discover the Master's touch in your own life, whatever labels or limitations you may face.

FOREWARD

There are moments in life when the noise of the world grows deafening—when confusion, chaos, and hardship blur our view of what truly matters. But then, something quiet and unmistakable happens: a divine touch, a whisper of grace, a shift in the atmosphere that reminds us we are not alone, that we are seen, and that we are uniquely designed.

The Master's Touch is more than a title—it is a testament. A reminder that the hands that shaped the stars are the same hands that reach gently into our lives, healing wounds we never thought would close, guiding paths we feared to walk, and lifting burdens we thought we'd carry forever.

In these pages, you'll discover stories, insights, and truths that reflect God's tender yet powerful movement in the hearts of His people. Pastor Gillard transparently shares his greatest hardships and challenges and what he has discovered that changed his life forever. Whether you are walking through a season of triumph or trial, this book invites you to experience the nearness of Christ in a way that is personal, transformative, and deeply real.

As you read, don't rush. Let the words settle. Let them speak. Because the same Master who touched the blind and made them see who touched the leper and made him clean, longs to touch your life too — with purpose, peace, and power.

May your heart be open. May your spirit be stirred. And as you read on, may you discover that, like Kenneth, you are a masterpiece because you've been touched by the master.

With anticipation and hope,

Dr. Ruben West

World Civility Ambassador

INTRODUCTION: THE DAY I FOUND MY NAME

"You have ADHD," the doctor said.

At 37 years old, those four letters explained my entire life. The special education classes in first grade. The jobs I couldn't keep. The college courses I couldn't pass despite my best efforts. The constant feeling that I was different but never understanding why.

I sat in that office, tears streaming down my face—not tears of sadness, but of relief. Finally, there was a name for what I'd been experiencing all these years. It wasn't that I was slow. It wasn't that I was stupid. I just learned differently. And in that moment, the Master's touch on my life became clearer than ever before.

For as long as I could remember, I'd struggled with reading, writing, and comprehension. As a boy, I would pray every night, "God, please make me smart. Please help me understand like the other kids." I dreamed of waking up one morning and suddenly being able to read without struggle, to follow directions easily, to remember what I'd just learned.

That prayer followed me from childhood into my teen years, through failed attempts at college, through job losses and setbacks, through a constant sense that I wasn't measuring up to what others expected of me — or what I expected of myself.

But that day in the doctor's office changed everything. It didn't suddenly make reading easier or erase the challenges I faced. But it gave me understanding. It gave me context. Most importantly, it showed me that what I had seen as a curse was actually part of God's unique design for my life.

You see, the very struggles that had caused me such pain had also developed in me a compassion for others who felt misunderstood or mislabeled. The limitations I faced in traditional education had forced me to develop other strengths — people skills, work ethic, determination, faith. The detours in my journey had actually been directing me toward my purpose all along.

That's what I call "the Master's touch" — God's hand guiding even our challenges toward our calling. It's the divine fingerprint on every part of our lives, even the parts that don't make sense to us at the time.

In the pages that follow, I want to take you on a journey — from my birth as a stillborn baby who wasn't breathing, through my struggles in school, my adoption into a loving family, my resistance to God's call, my diagnosis with ADHD, and the ministry that has given purpose to my pain.

But this book isn't just about my story. It's about yours too. Whatever labels have been placed on you—by others or by yourself — I want you to know that they don't define you. Whatever limitations you face, they don't determine your destiny. The Master who touched my life is touching yours too, weaving even your challenges into a purpose that only you can fulfill.

As my mother always told me, and as I now tell you: You can do it.

Let's discover how together.

HOW TO USE THIS BOOK

Each chapter of this book tells part of my story while offering principles you can apply to your own journey. To get the most from these pages:

1. **Read with an open heart.** My story may be different from yours, but the principles of overcoming labels and limitations apply to everyone.

2. **Pay attention to the "Master's Touch Moments."** These highlighted sections identify key turning points where I recognized God's hand guiding my journey.

3. **Consider the reflection questions** at the end of each chapter. Take time to write your answers or discuss them with a trusted friend.

4. **Apply the five-step process** outlined in Chapter 10 to your own challenges. These practical steps have helped me, and many others move beyond limitations.

5. **Share your insights.** Growth happens best in the community. Consider reading this book with others who are on a similar journey.

6. **Find your unique connection to your Creator.** Everyone has their own path to tread.

My prayer is that these pages will help you recognize the Master's touch in your own life — past, present, and future.

Each chapter will begin with a Scripture relating to the information contained within, as well as a direct quote from the Author's journal.

CHAPTER 1:

NOT BREATHING—THE FIRST TOUCH

THE BEGINNING

On February 8, 1962, I entered this world as a four-pound premature stillborn baby boy. When I came out of my birth mother's womb, I wasn't breathing.

So in my mind, I look back and I now realize, GOD TOUCHED ME!!!!! He gave me life."

> *"Before I formed thee in the belly I knew thee; and before thou camest forth out of the womb I sanctified thee."* — Jeremiah 1:5

I was born dead.

The doctors worked frantically. And then, something happened. Air filled my lungs. My heart started beating. Life came into me.

That was the first time — but certainly not the last — that I felt what I now call "the Master's touch." God touched me then, and I started breathing. He gave me life when death seemed certain.

This moment set the pattern for everything that would follow.

I didn't learn this story until decades later. I didn't understand that my struggles with learning, attention, and processing information connected back to those first fragile moments. But the Master knew. And those early struggles were preparing me for a purpose only I could fulfill.

A FAMILY BORN INTO STRUGGLE

My birth mother, Margaret Nell Prince Skelton, was just 21 years old when I was born — her fifth child. My birth father was Raymond Skelton Shine. I was one of eight children in this family.

The circumstances weren't ideal. My therapist would later tell me I was "conceived in struggle." Whatever was happening during my mother's pregnancy — whether substance use or emotional distress — affected my development.

For the first year and a half of my life, I was in and out of the hospital. I had a heart murmur and a twisted hip. I wore braces day and night. Doctors wanted to put me on nerve pills, but my foster Mother Effie Gillard said NO!

I survived those early challenges. Despite being born not breathing, despite the health issues, I lived. The Master wasn't finished with me yet.

FINDING A HOME

In the winter of 1964, at about eighteen months old, I was placed in foster care with Mrs. Effie Gillard.

Effie Myrtle Bridges Gillard was born in 1910. By the time I came into her life, she was in her fifties—a widow with grown children. She owned her own home, and her mother, Ella Mae Coleman, born in 1882, lived with her. Together, these remarkable women created the foundation that would shape my life.

Mrs. Gillard was known for having a big heart and opening her home to children who needed her. In 1942, she adopted my sister Marsha as a newborn. In 1946, they both moved to Flint and Mrs. Gillard became one of the first Black foster care mothers in the area.

The Gillard home at 2209 Howard Avenue became my world—a place filled with love, structure, and faith. It was where I was taught values, respect, and the importance of hard work. It was where, despite whatever limitations I might have, I was constantly told, "You can do it."

For nearly eight years, I was a foster child in this home—loved and cared for, but without the legal permanence that would make me fully part of the family. That changed in July of 1971, when I was nine years old.

THE ADOPTION

Mrs. Gillard decided she wanted to make it official. She wanted to adopt me.

This wasn't common in 1971. A single, widowed Black woman in her sixties adopting a nine-year-old boy wasn't something you saw every day. People tried to talk her out of it.

"There were people in the community and at our home church who told my mother, 'He's eight years old, another 10 years he will be 18. He came from a bad family. You have grown children, grandchildren. You are not married, you're widowed, you have your mother, you have your brother, now you want to adopt a son.'"

But my mother had a friend, the late Mrs. Pauline Todd who encouraged her: "I've raised two boys. You can raise Kenny."

And so, against all advice, my mother adopted me. I became Kenneth Rommel Gillard—her son, not just her foster child.

"That was the happiest day of my life. I was chosen from the beginning of time. I was chosen again by this gift, Mrs. Effie Gillard and Family."

Looking back, I see God's hand in this too. How many children born in my circumstances ended up with a permanent, loving home? The Master was touching my life through my mother's decision, setting me on a path I couldn't yet see.

MASTER'S TOUCH MOMENT

Sometimes God works through the decisions of others. My mother's choice to adopt me against all advice wasn't just her decision—it was divine intervention working through human hands. The Master touched my life by placing me exactly where I needed to be.

A FOUNDATION FOR LIFE

In the Gillard household, there were clear expectations:

"In her home, we knew that we were going to school, we knew we were going to go to church, we knew we were going to work, and we knew we were going to treat people with respect."

Those four pillars—education, faith, work ethic, and respect for others — became the foundation of my life. My mother also bought a home in Daytona Beach, Florida where we would spend summers. This helped to expand my horizons beyond Flint, Michigan.

But the most important gift my mother gave me was constant encouragement. No matter what challenge I faced, no matter how many times I failed, no matter what labels others put on me, my mother would say, "You can do it, Kenny."

When I couldn't believe in myself, she believed in me. When I couldn't see my potential, she saw it. When I couldn't imagine a future beyond my limitations, she imagined it for me.

That's the power of one person's faith in you—it can carry you until you learn to have faith in yourself.

THE FIRST LABEL

Despite my mother's love and encouragement, my early school years revealed that something was different about me. I didn't learn like other children. I struggled to read, to write, to understand directions, to sit still, to focus.

In the fall of 1968, I started first grade at SS Stewart Elementary School. I remember my teacher clearly, though the memories aren't all pleasant.

"I was told that when the teacher would leave the room, I would have the class in an uproar, and when she came back in,

the chaos was just too much for her to take."

And so, a decision was made that would affect the rest of my life: I was removed from the regular classroom and placed in special education.

"I can remember the feeling at that time. I was ashamed, bashful, and I felt like my friends who I went to school with were looking at me differently, even at the age of seven years old."

My special education teacher was Mrs. Sadie Thomas. She was kind, but the change was jarring. I went from being in a class of about 25 students on the A wing to being in a much smaller class on the B wing with children who seemed very different from me.

"I was treated nice but I can remember that I wasn't liked. The kids that were in the room that was around me, they really seemed different. It wasn't what I was used to."

That's when the names started—"slow," "special ed kid." That's when the pointing and whispering began. That's when I first felt the weight of being labeled by others, of being put in a box that didn't seem to fit who I thought I was.

I didn't understand why this happened until decades later. I didn't know that being born premature and stillborn had affected my brain development. I didn't realize that what they now call ADHD was shaping how I experienced the world and processed information.

All I knew then was that I was different. And different, in the eyes of a seven-year-old boy, felt deficient.

But even then, the Master was working. He was preparing me through this early experience of being labeled to one day reach others who felt the same way. He was teaching me compassion through my own pain. He was building in me a determination that would eventually become my strength.

I just couldn't see it yet.

PERSONAL REFLECTION

When I reflect on Jeremiah 1:5 — "Before I formed thee in the belly I knew thee"—I'm struck by the profound truth that God knew me before I took my first breath. He knew I would be born stillborn. He knew I would struggle with learning. He knew I would be moved to special education and feel the pain of being labeled "different."

None of this was accidental. None of this caught God by surprise. Before I was conceived, He had sanctified me for His purpose — a purpose that would require these very experiences to fulfill. The challenges that seemed so random and unfair were actually part of His intentional design.

I didn't understand this as a seven-year-old sitting in Mrs. Thomas's classroom, feeling ashamed and different. I couldn't see how God was forming me for a ministry that would reach others who felt labeled and limited. But He knew. Before I was in my mother's womb, He knew exactly who I would become and what I would need to experience to get there.

This is the comfort and challenge of Jeremiah 1:5. God doesn't just know us; He designs us—every detail, every challenge, every struggle—for a specific purpose that only we can fulfill. What feels like limitation to us is simply preparation in His hands.

REFLECTION QUESTIONS

1. Have you ever felt "different" in a way that caused you pain? How has that experience shaped you?
2. Who has been a source of encouragement in your life when you faced challenges?

3. Can you identify a difficult circumstance that later proved to be preparation for something important?
4. What "labels" have others placed on you that you're still working to overcome?
5. Where do you see divine intervention — the "Master's touch"— in your early life experiences?

CHAPTER 2:

THE BOY WHO FAILED

"I didn't know it at that time, but I was a visual learner. I would watch those men do things. And then in turn, I would do it."

"Train up a child in the way he should go: and when he is old, he will not depart from it." — Proverbs 22:6

DISCOVERING A DIFFERENT WAY

While textbooks confused me, I discovered I could learn by watching.

This became my survival strategy. I might not understand written instructions for shining shoes or waxing cars, but show me once, and I could replicate it perfectly.

Every night, I prayed: "God, please make me smart." I imagined waking up one morning able to read fluently and understand quickly like my classmates. That miracle never came—at least not in the way I expected. Instead, God began developing alternative strengths that would later define my ministry.

THE VILLAGE THAT RAISED ME

After my adoption in 1971, something remarkable happened. My mother went to our new pastor, Roy I. Greer, and said simply, "I just adopted a son and I need help."

His response changed my life: "The men of the church will be his father. We will help you with your son."

The men of Mount Olive Baptist Church surrounded me. From Pastor Greer as well as brother JT Williams, I learned faith and leadership.

From my neighborhood; Mr. James Wilson taught me auto repair. Mr Funderburk taught me how to wax and detail cars. From Deacon Nolan Adams, I learned to shine shoes and how to dress properly.

"Those men put their arms around me. Mr. Funderburk would wax his cars and take a toothbrush and get in between the doors. All those things, I do to this day."

These men didn't know they were accommodating my visual learning style. They just saw a boy who needed guidance and gave it by showing rather than telling. Through them, the Master was preparing me by teaching me to learn in ways that worked with my mind, not against it.

PURSUING DREAMS THROUGH CLOSED DOORS

Despite my struggles, I had dreams. I wanted to be a mortician. At age 12, I wrote to the Board of Mortuary Science. After graduating from Flint Central High School in 1980, I enrolled at Mott College to pursue this dream.

But college magnified my challenges. The reading load overwhelmed me. Writing assignments confused me. Tests defeated me.

"I went to three colleges and failed all three. I went to Mott Community College for mortuary science. I failed . I went to Baker College for business. I failed. I was accepted to ABT Seminary in Nashville, January 1985. I did one semester, but I failed again."

I couldn't understand why school was so difficult when work came so naturally. Why could I excel at practical tasks but fail at academic ones? Why did information that others absorbed easily seem to slip through my mind like water through fingers?

Each failure reinforced the labels. Each closed door seemed to confirm what I'd been told—that I was slow, limited, incapable.

MASTER'S TOUCH MOMENT

Often God redirects us through closed doors. What seemed like failure was actually protection—keeping me from paths that weren't aligned with my true purpose and unique design. The Master was touching my life even in rejection.

FINDING DIGNITY IN WORK

What saved me during those years was work. When academic achievement eluded me, I discovered dignity and purpose in serving others.

My first job was volunteering at Saint Joseph Hospital at age 16. Every Saturday, I helped patients, made beds, and distributed water from room to room. I loved knowing I was making a difference.

"I just didn't realize it. In January 1979, I became a volunteer at Saint Joseph Hospital every Saturday. I really enjoyed volunteering. I met a lot of good people."

In 1979 I was hired at Hurley Medical Center, where I worked as a student helper. But in 1982 a new requirement was implemented: all student helpers needed a 2.5 GPA. I had a 1.5. I proceeded to lose the job I loved.

After losing my position at Hurley, I found other work. I became the part-time janitor at Mount Olive Baptist Church — a position I would hold for over 30 years. I drove for Metro Medical Labs, delivering specimens across Michigan. I worked at Meijer's Thrifty Acres in sporting goods and at Kessel Foods as a bagger, eventually becoming a cashier.

"I was the slowest cashier at this particular time. The customers would wait in my line no matter how long it took. They always would tell me, 'You are a very nice young man and we like you.'"

Through these jobs, I developed something crucial: a strong work ethic and exceptional people skills. I found worth in what I could do, not what I couldn't. I discovered that while books might confuse me, people never did. I had a natural ability to connect, to serve, to make others feel valued.

God was laying groundwork I couldn't yet see — developing in me the character and skills I would need for ministry, even as I continued to resist that calling.

THE SEARCH FOR IDENTITY

At age 18, my mother suggested something that would help me begin to answer the questions I'd carried since childhood: Who am I? Why am I different?

We went to the probate court, and because my mother worked there, they quickly found information about my birth parents. My biological mother was in prison. They gave us her name, my father's name, and my grandmother's address.

"I met my biological grandmother and five of my siblings. A week or so later, I met my dad."

It was strange to look at people who resembled me but were essentially strangers. I learned I was one of eight children — my birth mother's fifth child, born when she was just 21 years old.

Meeting my birth family added another layer to my understanding, but it didn't explain why I struggled so much with learning. That revelation was still years away.

Throughout my twenties, I continued working various jobs, serving in various areas of the church, and wrestling with a sense that God was calling me to something I wasn't ready to accept. I still felt different, still struggled with reading and comprehension, still wondered why things that seemed simple for others were so difficult for me.

Yet even in my confusion, the Master was guiding me — using every experience to shape me for a purpose I couldn't yet see. Through it all, my mother's words sustained me: "You can do it, Kenny. You can do it."

I just had to keep believing her until I could believe it myself.

PERSONAL REFLECTION

Proverbs 22:6 instructs us to "Train up a child in the way he should go: and when he is old, he will not depart from it." As I look back on my childhood, I see how profoundly this scripture shaped my life — though not in the way most people interpret it.

The key phrase is "in the way he should go"— not in the way all children should go, but in the way that particular child is designed to go. My mother and the community around me didn't try to force me into a standard mold. They recognized my visual learning style and trained me accordingly. The men of Mount Olive showed rather than just told. My mother encouraged rather than demanded.

They were training me in my way—the way God designed me to learn and grow. They were acknowledging my unique design even before any of us understood why I was different.

When I didn't succeed in traditional education, this training sustained me. When doors closed, the values they instilled guided me to open new ones. When I felt like giving up, their words echoed in my spirit: "You can do it."

This is the deeper wisdom of Proverbs 22:6. Training a child isn't about forcing conformity; it's about recognizing and nurturing divine design. It's about preparing each unique individual for their specific purpose. And when we're trained according to our design, even when we struggle or stray, we have a foundation to return to—a path specially marked for our particular journey.

REFLECTION QUESTIONS

1. What labels have others placed on you that you've had to overcome?
2. Has there been a time when what seemed like failure actually redirected you toward your true purpose?
3. Who have been the key mentors in your life who taught you by showing rather than just telling?
4. How have your work experiences shaped your sense of identity and worth?
5. In what areas of your life do you need to hear and believe "You can do it" right now?

CHAPTER 3:

THE WORK OF YOUR HANDS

"My grandmother said this: what's in your head is good, but there are times you're gonna have to use your hands."

> *"And whatsoever ye do, do it heartily, as to the Lord, and not unto men."* — Colossians 3:23

FINDING DIGNITY IN WORK

When traditional education failed me, work saved me. When doors to college degrees and professional careers closed, God opened other doors—doors to meaningful labor that suited my unique design.

This wisdom became a cornerstone of my life. While my mind might struggle with reading and writing in conventional ways, my hands were capable of work that brought dignity, purpose, and provision. Throughout my life, even as I wrestled with undiagnosed ADHD, I discovered that work—honest, diligent work—was a pathway to self-respect and independence.

My work journey began early. At age 16, I started volunteering at Saint Joseph Hospital. Every Saturday, I would go in, assist patients, make sure they had water, make beds, and sometimes just talk to them. I didn't get paid, but I got something more valuable—confirmation that I could contribute, that I had something to offer, that I could make a difference.

"I really enjoyed volunteering at Saint Joe. I met a lot of good people at 17 years old."

That volunteer experience led to my first paid position at Hurley Medical Center in July 1979. I worked in dietary, preparing meal trays and eventually delivering them to patients. Again, I discovered I had a natural ability with people—a gift for making connections, for bringing comfort, for serving with genuine care.

When I lost that job due to academic requirements I couldn't meet, I found other ways to work. I cut grass. I washed cars. I cleaned houses. I shoveled snow. I found dignity in labor that others might have seen as menial but that I saw as meaningful.

"I was a hard worker, and I did what I could do to make it in life. Whatever I had to do, I would always do my very best."

My oldest sister Lee gave me advice I've carried throughout my working life:

"Whenever you do work for anybody, always remember you're doing the work for your mom." Since I would always want to do my best for my mother, this perspective ensured I gave my best effort to every job, no matter how small it might seem.

Work became not just a way to earn money but a way to express my values, to contribute to my community, to find purpose even when academic and professional doors remained closed.

THE ENTREPRENEURIAL SPIRIT

As I grew older, I discovered an entrepreneurial spirit within me. Rather than waiting for employers to overlook my learning challenges and hire me, I created my own opportunities.

These weren't just jobs to me. They were relationships with people. I served seniors who had once taught me in Sunday School. I washed cars for church members who had encouraged me as a child. I shoveled driveways for neighbors who had watched me grow up. The work connected me to my community in ways that transcended the financial transaction.

I discovered I had business skills that no classroom had taught me. I knew how to provide quality service. I understood the importance of reliability. I recognized the value of personal connection. I saw opportunities where others might not have looked.

My experiences taught me that work isn't just what you do with your hands—it's how you approach life. It's showing up consistently. It's doing your best even when no one is watching. It's finding ways to serve that play to your strengths rather than highlighting your weaknesses.

MASTER'S TOUCH MOMENT

When I was about 30, I was washing Mrs. Dunn's car—a church member who had known me since childhood. As I carefully detailed the interior, she watched me from her porch. *"Kenneth," she called, "the way you take care of that car tells me something about your character."* That simple observation helped me see that work wasn't just about the task; it was about how I approached it. The Master was teaching me that excellence in small things prepares you for excellence in great things.

THE BUS DRIVER

In 1992, a friend named Marcus Motley told me about job openings for bus drivers at the Mass Transportation Authority (MTA) in Flint. I applied and hoped for the best. Diana Thompson was the head of MTA Personnel. 5 minutes after my interview she called my house and talked to my mother. I was excited to learn that I was accepted. Diana also told me that I still needed to get my Commercial Driver's License (CDL).

Achieving this license presented a familiar challenge — a written test that my ADHD made extremely difficult. I spent five hours at the Secretary of State office, struggling with the questions, and ultimately failed. I went home discouraged and in tears.

My mother encouraged me to go back, and I did. There was a nice lady there who worked at the Secretary of State office. She told me, 'I saw you this morning having difficulties with the test. Let's try listening to the questions.' And I did listen, and I passed the test.

This simple accommodation — having someone read the questions to me instead of struggling to read them myself — made all the difference. It wasn't that I didn't know the material; it was that my brain processed written information differently.

Once I passed the test, I discovered I was a natural driver. For eight years, I drove bus routes throughout Flint, connecting with passengers from all walks of life, navigating challenging situations, developing confidence in my abilities.

"I learned the city of Flint, and again, I met some wonderful, wonderful people and students during this time."

One particular moment stands out from my training. My instructor, John Edmonds, was teaching me to navigate intersections with other vehicles.

We pulled up on Lippincott making a right turn onto Howard Street. There was a car at the stop sign, and I was waiting for the car to move. My instructor John said to me, 'Which vehicle is bigger? The bus or the car?' I said the bus. Mr. Edmund said to me, 'I better not ever see you pull up to a corner and wait on a car. You are the bigger vehicle, you have the right of way. You take charge and drive this bus!'"

That lesson became a metaphor for my life— learning to recognize my own "right of way," to move forward with confidence despite obstacles, to take charge of the vehicle God had given me to drive through life.

The MTA job became the best employment experience of my life up to that point. It gave me financial stability, developed my confidence, honed my people skills, and provided a platform for ministry outside the traditional church setting. Let no one tell you that working for the MTA is beneath you. It actually MADE ME.

WORKING WITH LIMITATIONS

In January 2000, I began feeling sleepy while driving the bus. I took action after a passenger alerted me to this. I reported it to my doctor that week. Dr. Michael Boucree took me off the road immediately and ordered tests to determine what was happening.

After seeing the results, Dr Boucree recommended that seeing a therapist would be the next logical step to take in order to find out what was going on with me.

Dr Bourcree suggested that perhaps I had built a wall that protected me from the hurt and disappointment I received from people and life. He said "Ken, we have to get this wall down".

So I took the advice from my family doctor. In March of 2000 I started therapy with Dr. Bates.

This led to my ADHD diagnosis and the beginning of realization to the truth behind all of the challenges I had experienced in my life. It also meant the end of my career as a bus driver—a job I had loved and excelled at for eight years.

Losing this position was painful, but it opened the door to a new understanding of myself and a new chapter in my ministry.

Sometimes God closes doors not as punishment but as redirection.

Throughout my working life, I've had to learn how to work with my limitations rather than against them. I've had to develop systems, find accommodations, and create environments that support my success.

"I discovered that I operate well when there is order in my life."

Order became essential to my functioning. I learned that my closet needed to be organized; my garage needed to be arranged systematically; my home needed to be clean and orderly. This wasn't just a preference; it was a necessity for my brain to function optimally. I learned that I don't function well in chaos.

I also discovered that consistency helped me succeed. Going to the same places, developing relationships with the same people, establishing routines that worked for me—all of these strategies helped me navigate a world that wasn't designed for how my brain works.

These weren't crutches; they were tools. They weren't signs of weakness; they were strategies for success. *Learning to work with my limitations rather than denying them or being defeated by them became one of the most important skills I developed.*

THE MINISTRY OF WORK

Through all of my work experiences, I came to understand that work itself can be ministry. It doesn't have to happen in a church building or with a clerical collar. It can happen on a bus, in someone's yard, while washing a car, or in any context where we serve others with excellence and integrity.

" The word also tells us man looks at the outward appearance, but God looks at the heart. It's my heart that makes connections with special people on this earth. It's my heart that leads and guides me. It's my heart. It's my spirit that continues to hold me, continues to mold me."

This understanding transformed how I viewed every job I held. Driving the bus wasn't just transportation; it was caring for people who needed to get to work, school, the doctor, or the grocery store. Cutting grass wasn't just yard maintenance; it was honoring seniors by maintaining their homes when they no longer could. Washing cars wasn't just cleaning; it was attention to detail that showed respect for the owner.

Even after I began formal ministry, this perspective continued to shape me. For over 30 years, I served as the part-time janitor at Mount Olive Baptist Church. Some might have seen this as beneath a minister, but I saw it as an integral part of my service to God and His people.

"I learned a lot about church work that summer. Well, at the end of summer, the janitor got sick, and they needed a part-time janitor. Pastor Greer said, 'Ken can do it,' and from 1982 to 2014, I was the part-time custodian of the Mount Olive Baptist Church, the youngest janitor in the history of that church."

This role taught me humility, service, and attention to detail. It gave me practical knowledge of the church building and operations. It connected me with members in ways that might not have happened if my only role had been preaching on Sundays.

MASTER'S TOUCH MOMENT

One Sunday morning, I arrived early to prepare the sanctuary as I always did. As I was carefully arranging the communion cups, Pastor Greer walked in. He watched me for a moment, then said, "Kenneth, God prepares us for ministry in ways we don't expect. The care you take with these cups shows me He's preparing you to care for souls." That moment transformed how I viewed my janitor role—not as separate from ministry but as training for it. The Master was teaching me that all work done with excellence is preparation for greater service.

THE VOLUNTEER

For over 40 years, I've also been a volunteer. From my earliest days at Saint Joseph Hospital to my recent role at Beaumont Hospital, I've found purpose and joy in giving my time without expectation of payment.

Even in my darkest moments, work—particularly volunteer work—provided purpose and connection when I needed it most.

In 2023, after resigning from my role as Assistant Chaplain at the Genesee County Jail, I began volunteering at Beaumont Hospital. It wasn't a paid position, but it gave me purpose, structure, and the opportunity to continue using my gifts to serve others.

Even when I made mistakes — which my ADHD made more likely in paperwork situations — the way I treated people often compensated for those errors. While I might struggle with forms and procedures, I excelled at personal connection. This became my signature in every workplace — treating people with such genuine care and respect that it overshadowed any limitations I might have.

THE DIGNITY OF LABOR

Society often measures success by degrees earned, positions held, or money accumulated. For someone with my learning challenges, these conventional measures of achievement were largely inaccessible. But God showed me another measure of success—the dignity of honest labor, the value of serving others, the worth of work done with excellence regardless of its prestige.

"I had a lot of dreams. In 1980, I went up to the small mall in Flint and talked to the Army recruiter. I thought I would go to the Army. So I went to Detroit, spent the night, and they gave me a physical exam and a test. I did not pass the test, and they told me that I had bad knees, and so again, another setback in my life."

Fast forward to 1989. This is a story from my time working at Meijer's Thrifty Acres. It illustrates something important about how I approach people.

The manager of Sporting Goods, Mr. White, told me I had filled out the paperwork for a private gun sale incorrectly using the wrong form. He explained that this error could cost me my job.

Fortunately, the customer I had helped came back to the store and we redid the paperwork.

The customer said: "If you fire him, we're going to go to the store manager, and we're going to demand that Kenneth keep his job."

Every closed door hurt. Every rejected application stung. Every test I failed reinforced the negative labels I had internalized.

But each setback also pushed me toward what would become my true calling and purpose. The doors that closed directed me to the doors God intended me to walk through.

Work became the context in which I discovered my worth. Not because of what I achieved, but because of how I served. Not because of what I earned, but because of what I gave. Not because of the status of my position, but because of the integrity with which I filled it.

Readers, I want to encourage you today.

Philippians 4:13 says, 'I can do all things through Christ who strengthens me.' I just want you to know, my sisters, my brothers, no matter your age, or no matter your color, you can do it today."

This has become my message to others who feel limited or labeled — that your worth isn't determined by conventional measures of success. *That honest work, done with integrity and excellence, in the spirit of God, carries dignity regardless of its status in society's eyes.* That God uses all kinds of work, all kinds of service, all kinds of labor to shape us for His purposes.

The Master touched every job I held, every position I filled, every service I rendered — using each to prepare me for ministry in ways I couldn't have imagined. He was teaching me people skills through patient care. He was teaching me persistence through lawn maintenance. He was teaching me attention to detail through car washing. He was teaching me reliability through bus driving.

None of it was wasted. None of it was without purpose. None of it was beneath me or unworthy of my best effort. All of it was preparation for the unique calling God had placed on my life—a calling that required precisely the experiences, skills, and perspective I was gaining through work that some might have considered ordinary.

PERSONAL REFLECTION

Colossians 3:23 tells us to work "heartily, as to the Lord, and not unto men." For years, I misunderstood this verse. I thought it simply meant to work hard, to give good effort. But through my journey with ADHD and learning differences, I've come to understand it more deeply.

Working "heartily" isn't just about effort; it's about bringing your whole self—your unique design, your particular gifts, your distinct perspective—to whatever work God places before you. It's about recognizing that the way you approach work matters as much as the work itself.

When I drove the bus "as to the Lord," it transformed an ordinary job into sacred service. When I cleaned the church "as to the Lord," it elevated janitorial work to spiritual significance. When I washed cars or cut grass "as to the Lord," it turned simple labor into an expression of worship.

This scripture doesn't distinguish between types of work — professional or manual, white-collar or blue-collar, paid or volunteer. It simply calls us to pour ourselves fully into whatever our hands find to do, recognizing that ultimately, we serve Christ, not human employers or expectations.

In a society that often measures worth by credentials I couldn't earn, this verse gave me an alternative measure: the heart I brought to my work. And in God's economy, that measure matters most. Working "heartily, as to the Lord" made even the most ordinary tasks extraordinary because they were transformed by the spirit in which they were performed.

REFLECTION QUESTIONS

1. What work or service gives you the greatest sense of purpose and dignity, regardless of its status or compensation?

2. How might limitations you've experienced be directing you toward your unique purpose rather than preventing you from achieving it?

3. In what ways can you approach your daily work "heartily, as to the Lord," regardless of what that work might be?

4. What systems or accommodations might help you work more effectively with any limitations you face?

5. How has God used your work experiences—even seemingly ordinary ones —to prepare you for your calling?

CHAPTER 4:

THE CALL I COULDN'T ANSWER

"I remember at the age of 17 God calling me to preach, and I felt like I was not worthy to preach. I was not smart enough to preach. I didn't read very well. I did not write very well, and I just did not see how God could use me at that time in my life."

> *"Before I formed thee in the belly I knew thee; and before thou camest forth out of the womb I sanctified thee, and I ordained thee a prophet unto the nations." —* Jeremiah 1:5

THE FIRST WHISPER

I was seventeen years old when I first heard God calling me to preach.

The call came softly at first—a persistent nudge, a whisper in my spirit, a sense that God wanted something from me that I wasn't ready to give. It came while I was working at Hurley Medical Center, while I was attending Mount Olive Baptist

Church, while I was still trying to figure out who I was and why I struggled so much with learning.

How could I possibly be a preacher? Preachers had to read the Bible fluently. They had to write sermons. They had to stand before people and speak eloquently. They had to answer questions and explain complicated theological concepts.

I could do none of those things. Or at least, I believed I couldn't.

So I ran. I ignored the call. I tried to convince myself I had imagined it. I focused on my job, on my volunteer work, on anything but this unsettling sense that God wanted me to do the very thing I felt least qualified to do.

THE SECOND CALLING

The call didn't go away. It returned when I was in my early twenties.

"The next time I can remember a call to ministry was when I was 23 years of age. That's when I went to Nashville to seminary, again I did not feel that I had what it took to be a preacher."

I thought maybe education would help me feel qualified. Maybe if I got training, I could overcome my limitations. So I applied to the American Baptist Theological Seminary in Nashville, Tennessee, and was accepted. In January 1985, I arrived on campus, ready to try.

I did well in some ways. The faculty recognized my character and commitment. I received an achievement award typically given to fourth-year students—and I got it in my first semester. But academically, I couldn't keep up. I couldn't pass the courses. I couldn't maintain the grades needed to continue.

After one semester, I had yet again failed. Another door closed. Another failure confirmed what I already believed about myself — that I wasn't smart enough, that I couldn't succeed in traditional education, that my limitations were too great to overcome.

And with that failure, I once again pushed aside the call to ministry. If I couldn't even pass seminary classes, how could I possibly be a preacher? If I couldn't understand theological textbooks, how could I teach others about God?

I returned to Flint and continued with what I knew I could do well — working with my hands and serving others. But most of all, in my church, being faithful to God in many ways. I became engaged, though the relationship ended before marriage. I drove for Metro Medical Labs, worked at Meijer's Thrifty Acres, and eventually got a job at Kessel Foods.

Life moved forward, but that persistent call remained in the background, *waiting.*

THE TURNING POINT

In April 1992, at age 30, I could no longer ignore the call.

"We were at church, my mother and I. After the preacher was done with his message, my mother took me to the altar for prayer, and I remember my mother saying, 'My son is struggling with something.'"

My mother knew. She could see the battle within me—the resistance, the fear, the sense that God was pursuing me for something I didn't feel ready or worthy to do.

Two months later, I traveled to Pittsburgh, Pennsylvania, with my friend Pastor Keith Ireland for the National Baptist Congress of Christian Education. After one of our classes, we were walking downtown when something extraordinary happened.

"This man staggered up to me (clearly intoxicated) and said, 'In all your travels, preach God's word.' Pastor Keith looked at me and said, 'I guess you've received your call.' I said, 'Yes.'"

It was a moment of clarity — as if God had orchestrated this strange encounter to confirm what I had been running from for thirteen years. This time, I couldn't dismiss it or explain it away. This time, I had to respond.

When I returned home, I went to Pastor Greer and told him, "I accept my call to preach God's word."

His response was both encouraging and sobering: "As long as you and I are in this office, it's me and you, but when you go out and announce your call, it's you and God."

That was the turning point. After years of running, of doubting, of feeling inadequate, I finally surrendered to what God had been calling me to do all along.

On August 16, 1992, I preached my first sermon at Mount Olive Baptist Church. The sermon was titled "Who Are You Seeking- Matthew 6:33", and I was licensed to preach.

MASTER'S TOUCH MOMENT

Sometimes the Master's touch comes through persistence. God didn't give up on my calling, even when I tried to run from it. He kept pursuing me, kept confirming His purpose for me, until I finally surrendered. And in that surrender, I found the beginning of freedom from the limitations I'd placed on myself.

THE NEW STRUGGLE

Accepting my call to preach didn't suddenly make reading easier or writing clearer. It didn't erase my learning challenges or magically give me the education I lacked. If anything, it magnified my awareness of these limitations.

I remember standing in the pulpit, stumbling over scripture readings, mispronouncing words. I remember the congregation sometimes calling out the correct pronunciation. I remember the embarrassment of struggling with something that seemed to come so naturally to other ministers.

"I can remember one of the senior men at the time, Mr. Clyde Edwards Sr., would take me

aside and encourage me and also assist me in the pronunciation of the words."

For the first seven years of my preaching ministry, I relied heavily on my friend Reverend Cary Brassfield. He was a gifted minister with a strong academic background.

"For the first seven years of my preaching ministry, he helped me to write my own sermons. In other words, God would give me a thought and I would tell Reverend Cary. And we would go to the scripture and we would go back and forth about what the text was saying."

This arrangement helped me overcome my limitations in reading and writing, but it also reinforced my sense of inadequacy. I couldn't even write my own sermons without help. I couldn't fully interpret scripture on my own. I felt like less of a minister because of it.

Yet people responded to my preaching. They felt the authenticity. They connected with my passion. They were moved by God's word. Something powerful was happening despite my limitations—or perhaps because of them.

"I struggled back and forth for seven years but in my struggle, I prayed and asked God to help me to learn how to write my own sermon. And he did."

The breakthrough came in an unexpected way. I was paying my phone bill at AT&T when the store manager offered me a promotion—an iPad. What seemed like a small thing became a life-changing tool. The device had an app called Notes with a microphone button.

"I learned pretty quickly that I could press this mic button and all I had to do was speak. I did not have to worry about spelling, or commas. It would all be there for me."

Suddenly, I could speak my thoughts and the technology would convert them to written text. I could dictate sermons without worrying about spelling or grammar. I could capture the ideas God was giving me without the barrier of writing them down. For the last 15 years, I've prepared all my sermons this way—speaking them into existence rather than writing them.

This was another example of the Master's touch in my life—providing exactly what I needed, when I needed it, to fulfill the calling He had placed on me.

My limitations hadn't disappeared, but God had provided a way through them.

THE BUS DRIVER

While I was learning to navigate ministry with my learning challenges, God was preparing another significant turn in my journey. In 1992, the same year I accepted my call to preach, a friend told me about job openings for bus drivers at the Mass Transportation Authority (MTA) in Flint.

I applied and was accepted, but I needed to get my Commercial Driver's License
(CDL). I went to the Secretary of State office to take the test, and for five hours I struggled with the questions. I failed.

"I remember going home and my mother was there and I began to cry. My mother encouraged me to go back."

I returned to the office, where a kind woman who worked there recognized me from that morning. She offered to help by giving me a cassette of the questions so I could listen instead of having to read them myself. This accommodation made all the difference—I passed the test and got my license.

Driving for the MTA became the best job I'd ever had. For eight years, I drove routes throughout Flint, connecting with people from all walks of life, developing confidence and skills that would later serve me in ministry. The job taught me about the city, about people, about managing challenging situations—all preparation for what God had planned.

"I remember that one day my instructor John Edmonds was training me on a Lapeer Road route. We pulled up on Lippincott making a right turn onto Howard Street. There was a car at the stop sign and I was waiting for the car to move. My instructor John said to me, 'Which vehicle is the bigger? The bus or the car?' I said the bus. Mr. Edmund said to me, 'I better not ever see you pull up to a corner and wait on a car. You are the bigger vehicle, you have the right of way. You take charge and drive this bus!'"

That lesson became a metaphor for my life and ministry. I needed to stop waiting for my limitations to move out of the way. I needed to take charge and move forward with the bigger purpose God had given me, regardless of the obstacles.

THE BEGINNING OF UNDERSTANDING

In January 2000, something alarming happened. I started falling asleep while driving the bus. After one incident where a passenger had to alert me, I reported it to my supervisor. My doctor immediately took me off the road and ordered tests to figure out what was happening.

"I went through a battery of tests, sleep clinics, and more doctors. Finally, a therapist and a psychiatrist was assigned to me."

My primary physician, Dr. Michael Boucree, said something that would change my understanding of myself and my struggles since childhood: "We have to get this wall down." That statement started me on the road to therapy that has changed my life.

The years of defenses I had built up to protect myself had to be torn down... brick by brick.

In March 2000, I began therapy with Dr. Robert Bates. It was during these sessions that a lifetime of struggle finally started to make sense. Dr. Bates uncovered my birth records from Hurley Medical Center, which revealed I was a premature stillborn baby.

And then came the diagnosis that explained everything: ADHD.

"I was diagnosed ADHD. So my whole life changed. My life started to make sense as we continue to dig deep, discovering that there was a wall that was up that had been built in my childhood, in my teen years, and my young adult years."

Suddenly, all the pieces fit together. The struggles in school, the difficulty with reading and writing, the challenges with focus and attention — they weren't because I was stupid or slow or deficient. They were because my brain was wired differently. They were because of how I came into this world.

"Those eight years of me being in therapy, I learn I wasn't a curse, and that I was different not in a bad way, but in a good way."

Over the next eight years, Dr. Bates helped me tear down that wall "brick by brick." We unpacked the buried anger, guilt, shame, and low self-esteem I had carried for decades. We addressed the labels others had placed on me and I had placed on myself. We worked through the pain of feeling different, inadequate, less-than.

And in that process, I discovered something powerful: The very thing I had seen as my greatest limitation—my ADHD—was actually part of God's unique design for my life. It wasn't a curse; it was a gift that allowed me to connect with others who felt broken or labeled or misunderstood.

The Master had touched me from the beginning—from that first breath after being born stillborn. He had been shaping me, through my differences and challenges, for a ministry I couldn't have imagined. He had been preparing me to reach people who, like me, needed to know they were more than their limitations, more than the labels others had placed on them.

In this new understanding of myself, my ministry took on deeper meaning. I was no longer trying to overcome or hide my differences. I was embracing them as essential to my calling, as vital to my ability to connect with those who needed the message God had given me.

"You can do it." My mother's words, which had carried me through so many challenges, now became the core of my ministry to others. Because I had lived it. Because I knew it was true. Because the Master had proven it in my own life.

PERSONAL REFLECTION

God's ordination does not depend on our qualifications; it depends on His sovereign choice. I now understand that God ordained me as a pastor/teacher before I was born—not despite my learning differences but because of them. He knew that my struggles would give me a unique voice, a distinctive perspective, an ability to reach people that more conventional ministers might not be able to reach.

When God calls, He equips. Sometimes that equipping comes through technology, like the iPad that transformed my sermon preparation. Sometimes it comes through people, like my friend Reverend Brassfield, who helped me understand scripture. Sometimes it comes through experiences, like my diagnosis with ADHD that helped me make sense of my challenges.

The call I resisted for thirteen years wasn't a mistake. The pastor God ordained me to be wasn't the conventional preacher I imagined, but the unique voice He designed me to be from the beginning. My resistance wasn't about God's mistake in calling me; it was about my mistake in thinking I had to be like everyone else to answer that call.

REFLECTION QUESTIONS

1. Have you ever felt God calling you to something you didn't feel qualified to do? How did you respond?

2. What limitations or challenges in your life might actually be preparing you for your unique purpose?

3. Who has helped you navigate your challenges, as Cary helped Kenneth with his sermons?

4. How might technology or other tools help you overcome limitations you face?

5. What "walls" in your life need to be taken down brick by brick through healing and understanding?

CHAPTER 5:

BEHIND THE ORANGE JUMPSUITS

"I came home. I put my certificate in my folder, and I put my badge in my drawer. It stayed there for seven years."

> *"I was in prison, and ye came unto me."* — Matthew 25:36

A CERTIFICATE IN A DRAWER

In December 1992, just months after preaching my first sermon, I completed a training course through the Forgotten Men's Ministry Jail Chaplaincy program. I received a certificate endorsed by the Michigan Sheriffs Association, qualifying me to serve as a correctional volunteer minister. It was seven years before I put it to use.

Looking back, I can see the Master's timing at work. I wasn't ready yet. I needed to grow in my faith, develop as a minister, and most importantly, I needed to understand myself better before I could effectively minister to others. I needed to begin the journey of confronting my own labels before I could help others confront theirs.

God knew exactly when I would be ready. And when that time came, He orchestrated an encounter that would change the direction of my ministry.

THE DIVINE APPOINTMENT

In June 2000, I was presiding over a funeral at Mount Olive Baptist Church when I met Pastor Charles Dantzler. We exchanged phone numbers, not knowing how God would use this seemingly random connection.

One month later, on a Monday in July 2000, I received a call from Pastor Dantzler. "Would you be interested in joining me at the Genesee County Jail? That certificate that had lain dormant in my drawer for seven years was about to find its purpose.

My first day was intimidating. Pastor Dantzler had me sit at the back of the class to observe him.

Every Monday evening we had 40-50 young men to minister to.

"Well, to be honest, it was a bit overwhelming. The young men were very hyped. They really liked Pastor Dantzler's teaching."

I watched as these men in orange jumpsuits—men society had labeled as criminals, offenders, inmates—asked questions, cried, and talked openly about what had brought them to jail. I saw how Pastor Dantzler's teaching was affecting them, how the Word was freeing them even within those concrete walls.

"You could tell they were receiving the word. It was freeing them."

For five years, I was mentored by Pastor Dantzler. Gradually, he let me take on more responsibility—starting the class, leading prayer, sharing scripture, giving my testimony. He was preparing me to eventually lead on my own.

Then, in 2005, an opportunity arose. The jail needed someone to lead another class, but Pastor Dantzler didn't have time. He turned to me.

"He didn't have time to come into the jail for another class. And so he gave the class to me. I didn't think that I could do it. But he said I could."

In January 2005, I began teaching my own class at the Genesee County Jail. What started as an intimidating experience became one of the most meaningful parts of my ministry. For the next sixteen years, every Tuesday, I would walk through those doors to share God's word with men whom society had given up on.

MASTER'S TOUCH MOMENT

God's timing is always perfect. That certificate sat in my drawer for seven years until I was ready—until I had grown enough, learned enough, and was prepared to step into this ministry. The Master was orchestrating events behind the scenes, preparing me for a purpose I couldn't yet see.

MY FATHER'S WISDOM

In July 2000, as I was beginning my jail ministry, another significant development occurred in my life. My biological father and I began to develop a deeper relationship.

I had first met my father when I was 18, but we didn't really connect until I was 28. Now, after hearing me talk about how I was encouraging a friend to spend time with his dad, the Holy Spirit spoke to me: "You need to get to know your dad."

The next day, I went to where my dad worked. That was the beginning of a 22year relationship that would profoundly impact my life and ministry.

"I really got to know my dad, which led me deeper into knowing myself."

My father shared wisdom that would prove invaluable in my jail ministry. He had spent four years in prison himself, not for a crime he committed but taking the fall for his best friend. His experience gave him insights that he passed on to me.

"In July of 2000, my dad and I had developed a wonderful relationship. He told me: 'Son, don't be fooled by the orange jumpsuits. Those men can read you. If you're real, they'll be with you. If you're fake, they will kick you out the door.'"

My dad's counsel became the foundation for my approach to jail ministry. Be real. Be authentic. Don't pretend to be something you're not. These men, despite being incarcerated, had an uncanny ability to detect pretense. They needed genuineness more than they needed eloquence.

This advice resonated deeply with me. All my life, I had struggled with feeling like I needed to hide my limitations, to pretend I was something I wasn't. Now, my father was telling me that the very authenticity I had struggled to embrace was exactly what these men needed.

THE MEN BEHIND THE LABELS

For sixteen years, every Tuesday, I taught at the Genesee County Jail. I saw hundreds, perhaps thousands, of men come through my class. Each one had a story. Each one carried labels, both those that society had placed on them and those they had placed on themselves.

"I saw the men's hearts. And that's key. Not the clothes that they wear. Not the crime that they committed. But their hearts."

I learned that these men weren't so different from me. Many had grown up feeling different, misunderstood, limited by circumstances beyond their control. Many had struggled with learning in traditional settings. Many had faced labels that diminished their sense of worth and possibility.

"I've had many challenges in my adult life, not knowing what was internally going on in my head...These men taught me a lot about me."

I began to understand that my own experience with ADHD and learning differences had uniquely prepared me to connect with these men. I knew what it meant to be labeled. I knew what it meant to feel like I didn't measure up. I knew what it meant to struggle with things that seemed to come easily to others.

And because I knew these things from experience, I could speak to these men with an authenticity and understanding that beyond our different circumstances. I could offer them what had been offered to me—the hope that they were more than their mistakes, more than their limitations, more than the labels society had placed on them.

MIKE'S STORY

Among the many men I met in those sixteen years, one stands out particularly.

I met Mike in February 2009. He was in his late twenties and came to my class because another inmate had recommended it.

He said,

"Reverend Gillard, I didn't pay any attention to what you said for the last hour and a half… but the last thing that you said is what caught me. And it changed my life.

You said: "If you have a problem with where you are at in life… look in the mirror. It starts with you."

Mike proceeded to go back to his cell and in the next 6 months, read the Bible 6 times.

Mike had been stabbed earlier in 2002 by a man at a party. This defined his outlook on life. In 2009, he got into another fight at a bar, went home, got a gun, and then went back to get justice but was too drunk to load the gun. Instead, he hit the man with the empty gun. That situation landed him in the Genesee County Jail, where our paths crossed.

A few days after attending my class, Mike was released. He called me for directions to Mount Olive Church where we met 15 minutes later. This was the beginning of his life change. He accepted Christ the first Sunday he attended Mount Olive Church. I baptized him, and that began our mentoring relationship. Through the power of prayer and his faithfulness and his commitment to his new found faith. This led to his sentence being reduced from 6 years to 6 months.
BUT GOD!

He remains faithful and consistent.

"Today, he's a man of God. He is pastoring God's Word Ministries on the South side of Flint. And he's doing very, very well. He continues to pastor to this day."

Mike's transformation is just one example of what can happen when someone begins to see themselves as God sees them, not as society labels them. His journey from jail to pastoring his own church demonstrates the power of the Master's touch to completely transform a life.

THE TWO PATHS

In my sixteen years of jail ministry, I observed that men typically chose one of two paths during their incarceration:

The first path was anger.

These men would come to class but remain angry. They would challenge the teacher and other inmates, claiming religion was meaningless. But their bitterness was evident.

The second path was different:

These men learned while incarcerated that they were not defined by their circumstances or their mistakes. They read their Bibles. They asked questions. They wrote about their anger, their hurts, their pain, their challenges. This process opened them up to healing and transformation.

"Those that choose to go and walk with God and allow them to work on that bitterness, work on that anger, work on that shame, work on those issues, forgive the past, forgive that father, forgive that mother, that sister...they come out a better person. "

I saw men transform before my eyes — men who society had written off, men who had written themselves off. I watched them discover their worth, their potential, their purpose. I witnessed them reject the labels that had limited them and embrace a new identity based on who God created them to be, not what they had done or what had been done to them.

"When they got out, many of them went into their various skills. And I have many testimonies of men who chose the right path versus the left."

THE LESSONS LEARNED

My time in the jail taught me three crucial lessons:

"The first thing is you have to be genuine. Number two, you have to have a heart for the work that's set before you. And third: you have to have an ear to listen."

Being genuine meant not pretending to be someone I wasn't. It meant acknowledging my own struggles and limitations while also affirming my worth and potential. It meant treating the men with dignity and respect, seeing beyond their crimes to the hearts God had created them with.

Having a heart for the work meant approaching these men not as projects to be fixed but as people to be loved. It meant seeing their potential when they couldn't see it themselves. It meant believing in their capacity for change even when their own belief had faltered.

And having an ear to listen—this was perhaps the most important lesson. So many of these men had never been truly heard. They had been talked at, lectured to, ordered around, but rarely listened to with genuine interest and respect.

MASTER'S TOUCH MOMENT

One Tuesday evening, I was particularly tired and almost didn't go to the jail. Something urged me to push through my fatigue and show up anyway. That night, a young man approached me after class with tears in his eyes. "Pastor," he said, "I was planning to end my life tonight, but what you shared changed everything." I hadn't planned a message about hope or suicide prevention—I had simply shared what the Spirit laid on my heart. That moment showed me how the Master orchestrates even our obedience to simple promptings. My weakness became the channel for His strength exactly when someone needed it most.

"These guys came from good homes. But they didn't get the nurturing. They did not adhere to the teaching of their parents or their grandmother or what have you. It's not that it wasn't there, but they wanted to be accepted. They wanted to be known. They wanted to be in the in-crowd."

By listening—really listening — I learned their stories. I discovered that many of them came from situations similar to my own. Many had felt different or inadequate. Many had struggled with learning or attention. Many had sought validation in destructive ways because they couldn't find it in constructive ones.

And in listening to their stories, I found healing for my own. I found affirmation that my differences weren't defects but distinctions that uniquely qualified me for this ministry. I found purpose in the very challenges that had once seemed purposeless.

The Master had been touching all of it—my birth as a stillborn baby, my struggles with learning, my diagnosis with ADHD, my call to ministry despite feeling inadequate. He had been weaving it all together to prepare me for these sixteen years of Tuesday nights, sitting in a jail cell, sharing hope with men who desperately needed to hear that they were more than their worst mistakes.

FROM MINISTRY TO CHAPLAINCY

In July 2020, my jail ministry entered a new phase. After sixteen years of voluntarily teaching one class per week, I received a call from the head Chaplain.

He said to me, 'I believe the Lord is calling you to the Genesee County Jail to be my assistant Chaplain." I prayed about it and I accepted the job."

For the next three years, I served as Assistant Chaplain at the Genesee County Jail. The role expanded my influence and responsibilities beyond the weekly class I had taught for so many years.

This position had its own challenges. There were internal tensions within the chaplain's office. I connected well with some colleagues but struggled with others. At times, I felt discouraged, uncertain about the workplace dynamics.

"The relationship was not there. It didn't seem like a good workplace anymore. I could tell there was some prejudice going on, some self-

righteousness going on, people talking about others, so I was not very happy."

In 2023, a difficult situation arose involving an employee smuggling contraband into the jail. My name was brought up in connection with this situation, though I wasn't involved. The experience deeply affected me. After returning from vacation in August, I became ill from the stress and took a five-week medical leave.

I made the decision that my resignation was the only option.

Though my time as Assistant Chaplain ended sooner than I expected, the twenty years I spent in jail ministry—sixteen as a volunteer teacher and three as Assistant Chaplain—were among the most meaningful of my life. They allowed me to turn my own struggles into strength for others, my own experience with labels into liberation for men society had written off.

The Master had touched my life in countless ways—from that first breath after being born stillborn to the classroom in the Genesee County Jail where I taught every Tuesday for sixteen years. He had taken what others saw as limitations and transformed them into qualifications for a ministry only I could fulfill.

And in the process, I had learned perhaps the most important lesson of all: I wasn't defined by what I couldn't do, but by who God created me to be and how I chose to use the unique gifts He had given me.

PERSONAL REFLECTION

Matthew 25:36 records Jesus saying, "I was in prison, and ye came unto me." For years, I understood this scripture as a call to minister to those in prison—to see Jesus in the faces of the incarcerated and serve them as I would serve Him. But my sixteen years of jail ministry taught me a deeper truth.

He wasn't just speaking about our ministry to prisoners. He was speaking about His presence with them — and with us — in places of confinement. Not just physical prisons with concrete walls and metal bars, but the mental, emotional, and spiritual prisons that confine so many of us.

I had been imprisoned by labels long before I ever walked into the Genesee County Jail. I had been confined by limitations, by others' perceptions, by my own self-doubt. And in those prisons, Jesus had come to me—through my mother's encouragement, through mentors who believed in me, through a therapist who helped me understand myself.

When I taught those classes every Tuesday for sixteen years, I wasn't just ministering to inmates; I was ministering with them. I was sharing liberation I had found from my own confinement. I was testifying to how Jesus had come to me in my prison and set me free.

This is the transformative power of Matthew 25:36. When we visit those in prison —whether literal jails or metaphorical ones—we encounter Jesus. Not just in them, but in ourselves. Not just as givers of ministry, but as recipients of it. In my years of jail ministry, I received as much as I gave. I was as transformed as those I came to serve.

REFLECTION QUESTIONS

1. How has your own pain or struggle uniquely qualified you to help others?

2. Like Kenneth's father advised about the men in jail, where in your life do you need to be more "real" rather than pretending to be something you're not?

3. What labels have others placed on you that you're still allowing to limit your potential?

4. Where do you need to "look in the mirror" instead of blaming others for problems in your life?

5. How might the Master be preparing you, through current challenges, for a purpose you can't yet see?

CHAPTER 6:

THE FIVE STEP S FORWARD

"I've learned that I wasn't stupid, that I wasn't slow, I just learned differently. And so getting that title ADHD just opened my world up. And it began to help me to understand who I was."

"For I know the thoughts that I think toward you, saith the LORD, thoughts of peace, and not of evil, to give you an expected end." — Jeremiah 29:11

THE BREAKTHROUGH

The year 2000 marked a turning point in my life. Everything changed when I was diagnosed with ADHD at age 37.

For decades, I had struggled without understanding why. I had carried the weight of labels others had placed on me — "slow," "special ed kid," "not college material." I had internalized these labels, believing there was something fundamentally wrong with me, something I couldn't overcome no matter how hard I tried.

The diagnosis didn't instantly solve my problems. It didn't suddenly make reading easier or writing clearer. But it gave me something invaluable: understanding.

Through eight years of therapy with Dr. Bates, I unpacked the "buried anger, the very guilt, the madness, the shame." We took down the wall that had been built in my childhood, teen years, and young adult life—the wall of believing I wasn't good enough, smart enough, capable enough.

It took until my early 40s to fully unpack Kenneth Rommel Gillard.

This unpacking process was painful but necessary. I had to confront the hurt, anger, and shame I had carried for so long. I had to forgive those who had labeled and limited me. Most importantly, I had to forgive myself for believing those limitations defined me.

MASTER'S TOUCH MOMENT

During one therapy session when I was particularly discouraged, Dr. Bates pulled out my birth records. "Look at this," he said, pointing to my birth certificate. "You weren't breathing when you were born, yet you survived. You've been beating the odds since your first moments on earth." In that instant, I saw my life differently — not as a series of failures but as a miracle of persistence. The Master had been sustaining me from my very first breath.

Through this journey of healing and self-discovery, I developed a process for overcoming the obstacles of labels and limitations — a five-step approach that has helped me and many others move beyond what seemed like insurmountable barriers.

STEP ONE: ACCEPT YOUR DIFFERENCE

The first step toward overcoming limitations is accepting that we all have differences and challenges. Whatever yours may be, it's what makes you unique.

"ADHD is a GIFT for my life. I've met some wonderful people who have assisted me in my life. They make the difference."

For years, I saw my ADHD as a curse, a defect that made me less than others. Through therapy and personal growth, I came to see it differently—not as a disability but as a different ability. My brain processes information differently. I learn differently. I see the world differently.

And these differences aren't deficiencies—they're distinctions that equip me for unique contributions others might not be able to make.

"I now know that I am a man of consistency. I've also learned that I work best when things are in order. For instance, my closet needs to be in order, my garage. In fact, my entire home is clean, and I live in a pretty orderly place."

Understanding how I function best has allowed me to create systems and environments that support my success rather than fighting against my natural tendencies.

Accepting your difference doesn't mean resigning yourself to limitation. It means understanding yourself well enough to navigate life in ways that work with your unique design rather than against it.

STEP TWO: SEEK HELP

For me, intensive therapy was a life-changing experience. You may greatly benefit from counseling, a life coach, mentoring, or tutoring. Find someone who will be in your corner, supporting and encouraging you to live your best life.

"I would recommend therapy at the top of the list. Get to understand who you are. Don't wear the label, but embrace who you are. Get to know who you are."

For eight years, I met regularly with Dr. Bates. No one made me go. I went willingly because I wanted to understand myself better, to break free from the limitations I had accepted for so long.

"I'm not going to tell you that it's not work. Eight years of therapy 20+ years ago, the last four years in therapy. I am better today for having such great therapists in my life to help me to deal with life's challenges, problems, issues."

Seeking help isn't a sign of weakness; it's a sign of wisdom. We weren't meant to figure everything out on our own. We need guides and mentors who can help us see what we can't see about ourselves, who can provide perspective and tools we might not discover alone.

In addition to therapy, I've sought help through technology. When an iPad with speech-to-text capability became available, it transformed my ability to prepare sermons. This was a tool that made all the difference.

Don't be afraid to ask for the help you need. Don't be ashamed to use tools and accommodations that level the playing field. These aren't crutches; they're bridges to your potential.

MASTER'S TOUCH MOMENT

Sometimes God's touch comes through other people's insights. Dr. Bates didn't just diagnose me—he helped me see myself as God sees me. In one session, he told me, "You weren't born disabled; you were born unique." That perspective shift was divine intervention working through human wisdom. It changed how I viewed myself and my purpose.

STEP THREE: STOP COMPARING

God made you uniquely you, and His plan is always perfect. Comparing yourself to others will only lead to discouragement and self-doubt.

"I've learned to read more and improve as I continue to grow older. I read more now than I ever have in my life. I encourage others to read; listen to videos. All this builds a strong sense of self."

For years, I compared my reading ability to others and always found myself lacking. I compared my academic achievements (or lack thereof) to friends who had gone on to college and careers requiring degrees. I compared my sermon preparation to other ministers who could easily read and write without assistance.

These comparisons never helped me grow; they only reinforced my sense of inadequacy.

When I stopped comparing myself to others and started focusing on my own growth—from where I was to where I could be—everything changed. I began to celebrate small victories instead of mourning that I wasn't where others were. I began to appreciate my unique strengths instead of fixating on areas where others excelled and I struggled.

Comparing yourself to others is a lose-lose proposition. If you come up short, you feel inadequate. If you come out ahead, you risk pride and complacency. The only healthy comparison is between who you were yesterday and who you are today—between who you are now and who God is calling you to become.

STEP FOUR: SURROUND YOURSELF WITH SUPPORTERS

If the only people in your life are those who whisper behind your back or criticize your weaknesses, those are toxic people. Get them out of your life and surround yourself with positive influences instead.

"I go to the same credit union, I have managers and tellers who know me and know how to assist me in my business. I have been going to the same cleaners for the last 32 years. They know me and I know them."

I've learned to build relationships with people who see me for who I am, accept me for who I am, and can encourage me to be better. These are people who know my shortcomings but also recognize my strengths.

"I have many, many spiritual sons and daughters that I have poured into for the last 25 years of my life. The mentor comes from the absence of that male influence in my life, but it also comes from the males that I did have in my life that influenced me. And in turn, it has

caused me to influence many, many young men in their lives."

Supportive relationships are reciprocal. As I've mentored young men, they have also sharpened me. As I've taught in the jail, the inmates have taught me valuable lessons as well. As I've pastored, my congregation has ministered to me in profound ways.

You need people who can speak truth into your life with love—people who don't just point out your weaknesses but help you develop your strengths, who don't just identify problems but help you find solutions, who don't just see you as you are but envision what you can become with God's help.

STEP FIVE: FORGIVE AND BE GRATEFUL

Forgive yourself and forgive others. Forgive yourself for the times you failed. Forgive those who set you up for failure. Then take the crucial next step: be grateful for every experience that shaped you.

"I had to learn that I must appreciate who I am. I believe that God knew I would be this way. And I believe that my life was designed this way."

Forgiving myself was perhaps the hardest part of my journey. I had to forgive myself for believing I was deficient when I was simply different. I had to forgive myself for the opportunities I had missed, the dreams I had abandoned, the times I had given up because I believed I wasn't capable.

I also had to forgive those who had labeled and limited me—teachers who moved me to special education without explaining why, college professors who couldn't accommodate my learning style, employers who judged me by standards that didn't account for my unique challenges.

But forgiveness alone isn't enough. True liberation comes when forgiveness gives way to gratitude—when we can actually thank God for the experiences that once caused us pain, recognizing how they've shaped us for our purpose.

"When I look back over my life, it's been very, very challenging. I remember Dr. Bates, my therapist over 20 years ago, told me that I was

conceived in struggle and in the womb I struggled and at birth stillborn, 4 pounds preemie was not breathing, a struggle, but God."

That "but God" is the turning point where forgiveness becomes gratitude. I'm now grateful for being born stillborn because it prepared me to understand what it means to receive life as a gift. I'm grateful for my learning challenges because they taught me compassion for others who struggle. I'm grateful even for the closed doors because they directed me to the open ones God had prepared.

Being grateful is directly acknowledging your acceptance of God's plan regardless of the circumstances. There is always something to be grateful for, which reconnects you to the divine within. When I look at my life through eyes of gratitude, I don't see a series of limitations and failures—I see a masterfully crafted journey leading me exactly where I needed to be.

Forgiveness without gratitude still keeps you tied to the pain. Gratitude transforms that pain into purpose. It says, "Not only do I release this hurt, but I now recognize it as essential to who I've become and what I can offer."

Forgiveness is a process, not a one-time event. I've had to forgive myself and others again and again as new insights emerged about how my early experiences shaped me. With each act of forgiveness, I've tried to find something to be grateful for—some way that even painful experiences were preparing me for my unique calling. This practice has freed me to move forward, to grow, to become more fully the person God created me to be.

THE TRANSFORMATION

As I've applied these five steps in my own life, transformation has occurred. The labels that once limited me no longer define me. The challenges I face with ADHD are still real, but they don't determine what I can accomplish.

I've discovered that while traditional education was difficult for me, practical skills and entrepreneurship come naturally. I've built businesses, served my community, and found dignity in work that plays to my strengths rather than highlighting my weaknesses.

"I had a lawn care service, where I cut a lot of lawns for seniors. I also cleaned homes for

some of the senior members in my community. I cleaned gutters. I also washed windows and washed houses down in the springtime. I also had a car cleaning business, it was called triple K.K.K (Kens Kar Kare). I blew and shoveled people's driveways in the winter. "

I've developed deep, meaningful relationships with people across generations who accept me as I am while encouraging me to grow. These relationships have been the context for both giving and receiving wisdom, for both teaching and learning.

"All I'm saying is that when I look back over my life, my 20s, my 30s, my 40s, my 50s, ADHD has played a significant part in my life. I didn't know what I was dealing with, and I still have my challenges even today. I'm just at a much better place in my life."

The transformation hasn't erased my challenges. I still have days when reading is difficult, when focus is elusive, when depression tries to creep in. The difference is that I now have tools, understanding, relationships, and most importantly, a perspective that allows me to navigate these challenges without being defined by them.

FROM PULPIT SUPPLY TO PASTOR

In November 2017, another unexpected door opened in my journey. I was invited to preach at Hill Road Baptist Church as pulpit supply—a guest preacher filling in when needed.

"I went to Hill Road Baptist church as a pulpit supply preacher in November 2017, and on February 2 2018, I became interim pastor. 14 months later on April 27, 2019 I was installed as the pastor of Hill Road Baptist church"

This progression from occasional preacher to interim pastor to full pastor wasn't something I had planned or pursued. It was another example of the Master opening doors I hadn't even thought to knock on.

What made this opportunity particularly significant was the nature of the congregation at Hill Road Baptist Church.

"Hill Road Baptist Church was in Grand Blanc near Swartz Creek. It was a white congregation. I was the first man of color to become a pastor of this church."

After years of feeling different because of my learning challenges, I was now different in another way—the first Black pastor of a predominantly white congregation. Yet this difference, like my ADHD, became not a limitation but a distinction that allowed for unique ministry opportunities.

For nearly four years, I pastored Hill Road Baptist Church, serving as a bridgebuilder and bringing perspectives that might not otherwise have been represented in that congregation. My experience with being labeled and limited gave me insight into crossing cultural and racial boundaries with grace and understanding.

This pastoral role became yet another way the Master used my unique experiences and challenges for His purposes. What might have seemed like disadvantages in some contexts became advantages in others. The very things that made me different equipped me for service that someone with a more conventional background might not have been able to offer.

THE JOURNEY CONTINUES

Today, at over 60 years old, I continue to navigate life with ADHD. It hasn't disappeared. It still presents challenges. But it no longer defines me or limits what I believe I can accomplish.

"I believe I have some things to do in this life before I leave this earth. I believe I have more assignments. I believe I have more preaching opportunities. I believe that I have some more speaking opportunities. I believe that I have to write this book and I believe that I'm gonna make it."

I've learned that my journey isn't just about overcoming personal limitations. It's about using my experience to help others overcome theirs. It's about turning what could have been merely personal pain into public purpose. It's about seeing the Master's touch in every aspect of my life—even and especially in the challenges —and helping others recognize that same divine fingerprint in their own lives.

"You have to know that you're bigger and better than the diagnosis. You have to be strong. You

have to persevere. You continue to push forward in this life."

That's the message I want to leave you with. Whatever labels have been placed on you — by others or by yourself—they don't define you. Whatever limitations you face — whether physical, mental, emotional, or circumstantial — they don't determine your destiny.

The Master who touched my life is touching yours too, weaving even your challenges into a purpose that only you can fulfill. Trust His design. Follow His lead. Embrace your unique calling.

You can do it.

PERSONAL REFLECTION

Looking back on Jeremiah 29:11, I now understand that God truly did have
"thoughts of peace, and not of evil" for me all along. What seemed like obstacles — being born stillborn, struggling with learning, facing closed doors in education and careers — were actually part of His intricate plan to shape me for a unique purpose.

When I was diagnosed with ADHD at 37, it wasn't the end of my story; it was the beginning of understanding how God's thoughts toward me had always been for good. The very challenges that caused me pain became channels of peace for others facing similar struggles. The label that seemed to limit me became the launching pad for a ministry that could reach people conventional approaches might miss.

I see now that the "expected end" God promised wasn't about making me like everyone else—it was about making me fully myself, the unique person He designed me to be. His thoughts toward us are always of peace, even when our path leads through difficulty. The Master touches every part of our journey, weaving even our weaknesses into the tapestry of His perfect plan.

REFLECTION QUESTIONS

1. Which of the five steps for overcoming limitations do you find most challenging, and why?

2. What unique strengths might be hidden within your greatest challenges or differences?

3. Who are the supportive people in your life who see your potential, and how can you strengthen those relationships?

4. What labels have you accepted as defining you that you need to reconsider?

5. Where do you see the Master's touch in the challenges you've faced in your life?

CHAPTER 7:

BUILDING YOUR CIRCLE

"One of the things you gotta have is real good healthy relationships, with people that are younger, your age, and older, who sees you for who you are, accept you for who you are, and can encourage you to be better."

> *"Iron sharpeneth iron; so a man sharpeneth the countenance of his friend."*
> — Proverbs 27:17

THE POWER OF RELATIONSHIPS

If there's one lesson I've learned through my journey with ADHD and learning differences, it's this: we cannot succeed alone. We need each other. We need people who see our potential, understand our struggles, and walk alongside us through both victories and setbacks.

My life has been shaped by relationships—with my mother and grandmother who believed in me when I couldn't believe in myself; with the men of Mount Olive who became my fathers when I had none; with Pastor Dantzler who mentored me in jail ministry; with Dr. Bates who helped me understand myself through therapy; with the inmates whose stories resonated with my own; with the young men I've been privileged to mentor.

These relationships weren't accidental. They were divine appointments—people God placed in my life at exactly the right moments to help me navigate challenges, overcome limitations, and discover my purpose.

Building your circle—surrounding yourself with people who support, challenge, and encourage you— *it is not just helpful; it is essential* . Especially for those of us who face unique challenges or who have been labeled and limited by others, having the right people around us can make the difference between giving up and pressing forward, between believing the labels and discovering our true identity.

"We were not put on this earth to be by ourselves. I believe we are put on this earth to build relationships with one another, connect,

build one another, encourage one another, and love one another."

IRON SHARPENS IRON

One of the most powerful principles I've discovered about relationships is captured in Proverbs 27:17: "Iron sharpeneth iron; so a man sharpeneth the countenance of his friend."

How do you describe "iron sharpening iron" when you're trying to tell people about the challenges that they might face in life?

True relationships aren't just about affirmation; they're about transformation. They're about becoming sharper, stronger, more effective through the friction and challenge of engaging with others who care enough to speak truth into our lives.

I experienced this first with my biological father. Though I didn't meet him until I was 18 and didn't truly connect with him until I was 28, we developed a significant relationship over 22 years until his passing.

My father sharpened me during this time. He challenged me. He gave me insights not just about life in general but about myself specifically. Through our relationship, I came to understand aspects of my identity and calling that might have remained hidden otherwise.

"He gave me his time, he gave me conversation, he gave me wisdom, and a lot of understanding about life."

I experienced this " *iron-sharpening-iron dynamic"* in other relationships as well. Pastor Dantzler mentored me in jail ministry for five years before entrusting me with my own class. He didn't just affirm me; he challenged me, corrected me, prepared me for effective service. At times it wasn't easy. *But I did listen.*

Dr. Bates provided both support and challenge during our eight years of therapy. He created a safe space for me to process pain and anger, but he also pushed me to confront hard truths about myself and take responsibility for my growth.

Dr Bates taught me to ask myself:

"Is it healthy or unhealthy … for me."

This simple idea helped me to make many future decisions in my life.

Another way to look at "iron sharpening iron" is as follows.

You are not only sharpening yourself, you are sharpening the other person as well.

This mutual sharpening is essential. It's not one person always giving and another always receiving. It's a reciprocal relationship where both individuals grow, learn, and become more effective through their interaction.

MASTER'S TOUCH MOMENT

A few years ago, I was mentoring a young man who was struggling with his own learning challenges. During one of our conversations, he made an observation that stopped me in my tracks. "Pastor Kenneth," he said, "have you ever noticed that you speak more clearly when you're teaching than when you're just talking?" I hadn't realized this, but he was right. The Master had given me eloquence specifically for the context of teaching and preaching—a gift I might never have recognized if this young man hadn't pointed it out. Sometimes God reveals aspects of His touch through the insights of those we're mentoring.

THE MENTOR BECOMES THE MENTEE

One of the most beautiful aspects of true mentoring relationships is that they're rarely one-directional. The mentor often becomes the mentee. The teacher becomes the student. The giver becomes the receiver.

This principle has been evident in my mentoring relationships with young men. While I've poured into their lives, they have equally poured into mine. They've taught me about contemporary culture, about new perspectives, about ways of thinking I might never have encountered otherwise.

I remember meeting my *'spiritual nephew'* from Nashville for the first time. After our initial meeting, we began talking regularly—two or three times a week.

Despite our age difference—I was in my sixties, he in his twenties—we developed a relationship that sharpened us both. He brought fresh perspectives and youthful energy; I brought life experience and spiritual insights. Together, we continue to grow in ways neither of us could have alone.

It's not about age or status or education. It's about genuine exchange, authentic sharing, and reciprocal growth. It's about recognizing that God speaks through people of all backgrounds, all ages, all walks of life.

THE CHURCH AS FAMILY

The church has been central to my understanding of relationships. From childhood, Mount Olive Baptist Church became my extended family—a community that supported, challenged, and shaped me.

The church became the context in which I learned about healthy relationships. It was where I observed marriages that worked, families that functioned well, friendships that endured. It was where I saw conflict resolved, differences reconciled, burdens shared.

Throughout all the challenges I faced, the church remained a constant—a family that didn't abandon me when I struggled, a community that continued to believe in me even when I failed. It became a model for the kind of relationships I would later develop with those I mentored.

When I eventually left Mount Olive after decades of membership to pursue my next spiritual assignment, it was painful. Yet the principles of relationship I had learned there transferred to new communities. These included: From The Heart Church Pastor G. Davis, then New Jerusalem Full Gospel Baptist Church under Pastor P. Sanders, and eventually Hill Road Baptist Church where I served as pastor.

In each context, I continued to build relationships that reflected what I had experienced at Mount Olive—authentic, supportive, challenging connections that promoted growth and healing.

THE ART OF MENTORING

Over the past 25 years, I've had the privilege of mentoring many young men. This wasn't something I set out to do initially. It emerged organically from my experiences and the recognition that I had something valuable to offer—not despite my challenges - but because of them.

I have many spiritual sons and daughters that I have poured my heart into for the last 25 years of my life. The mentor comes from the absence of that male influence in my life, but it also comes from the males that I did have that influenced me. And in turn, it has caused me to influence many young men in their lives.

I learned what young men need; both by what I missed and what I received. This has given me insights into how to connect with young men who might be struggling with their own sense of identity and purpose.

Names that come to mind include (but are not limited to) : Antoine, Keith, Artemis, Quinton, Baridi, Brad, Mike, Kevin, Trey, JT, James, Shawn, and a host of others.

Several principles have guided my mentoring relationships:

First, I focus on genuine connection.
Before offering advice or correction, I establish trust. I listen more than I speak. I create a safe space where young men can express their real thoughts and feelings without fear of judgment.

Second, I share my own struggles openly.
I don't present myself as someone who has it all figured out. I talk about my journey with ADHD, my failures in education, my challenges in ministry. This vulnerability creates a context in which others feel free to be vulnerable as well.

Third, I affirm potential while addressing challenges.
I help young men see who they can become while also being honest about what might be holding them back. This balance of encouragement and truth is essential for growth.

Fourth, mentoring is a long-term commitment.
It's not about quick fixes or simple solutions. It's about walking alongside someone through various seasons of their life, providing consistent presence and support even through setbacks and struggles.

Fifth, I maintain appropriate boundaries.
While mentoring involves genuine care and connection, it also requires wisdom about roles and responsibilities. I've learned to be close enough to influence without creating dependency, to care deeply without taking responsibility for another's choices.

MASTER'S TOUCH MOMENT

Several years ago, I was mentoring a young man who was struggling with anger and resentment toward his father who had abandoned him. During one conversation, I shared my own journey of meeting my biological father as an adult and the healing that came through that relationship. *As I spoke, I suddenly realized I was describing my experience differently than I ever had before—with new insights I hadn't previously articulated.* The Master was revealing aspects of my own healing even as I was trying to help someone else heal. That moment showed me how mentoring becomes a channel for God to work in both lives simultaneously.

BUILDING TRUST

Perhaps the most important aspect of building your circle is establishing trust. Without trust, relationships remain superficial. Without trust, iron cannot sharpen iron. Without trust, mentoring becomes mere instruction rather than transformation.

"You have to become comfortable with who you are and your uniqueness and /or your differences. People are going to talk about you no matter what. But you have to feel good about you. Because it has made you to be who you are: *today, yesterday, and tomorrow."*

Building trust begins with authenticity. In all my relationships — whether with peers, with those I mentor, or with those who mentor me — I've tried to be genuine. I don't pretend to be something I'm not. I don't hide my struggles or exaggerate my successes. I present myself as I am, with both strengths and weaknesses, both gifts and challenges.

This authenticity creates space for others to be authentic as well. When I'm honest about my journey with ADHD, it gives permission for others to be honest about their own challenges. When I acknowledge areas where I'm still growing, it allows others to acknowledge their growth edges too.

Trust also requires consistency. People need to know they can count on you— that you'll show up when you say you will, that you'll follow through on commitments, that your words and actions align.

"I'm told quite often I have a memory of an elephant, well I do, but I have learned to appreciate me. I've learned to appreciate the gifts that I have, the skills that I have, the assignments that are put before me. "

I've worked hard to be consistent in my relationships. Despite the challenges
ADHD can present with organization and follow-through, I've developed systems to ensure I keep commitments and remain reliable. This consistency has been essential in building trust with those I mentor.

Trust further requires genuine care. People can tell when your interest is superficial or when your motives are self-serving. They know when you're investing in them because you truly value them versus when you're using the relationship for your own purposes.

"I must admit I had a wonderful mother. My mother always encouraged me. In her home, we knew that we were going to school, we knew we were going to go to church, we knew we were going to work, and we knew we were going to treat people with respect."

The foundation my mother laid—especially regarding treating people with respect — has guided all my relationships. I've tried to approach each person I mentor with genuine care and respect, seeing them not as projects but as individuals of immense value and potential.

THE CIRCLE OF SUPPORT

While mentoring relationships have been central to my ministry, I've also needed my own circle of support—relationships with peers and mentors who provide encouragement, accountability, and perspective.

"I have found that those people are placed in those various positions to assist me and others in life. You have to become comfortable with who you are and your uniqueness and or your difference."

I've learned to identify people who see my potential, who understand my challenges, who believe in my calling. I've cultivated relationships with these individuals, being intentional about staying connected and vulnerable with them.

This circle of support has been diverse. It has included other ministers who understand the unique challenges of pastoral work. It has included friends from different backgrounds who bring varied perspectives. It has included professionals like Dr. Bates who offer specialized insights. It has included older mentors who provide wisdom and younger friends who keep me current.

The diversity of this circle has been important. Different relationships meet different needs. Some friends provide emotional support. Others offer intellectual challenge. Still others share spiritual insights. Some relationships are deeply personal, while others are more focused on ministry or community involvement.

"I also need to say that I am a man of consistency, but I've also grown to venture out to other cities, states, and I love traveling, and I've also learned that God has planted people all over the world for me, and my uniqueness. I just have to be open to receive."

This openness to relationships in various contexts has enriched my life and ministry. It has helped me avoid the insularity that can develop when we limit ourselves to relationships with people just like us. It has exposed me to different ways of thinking, different approaches to challenges, different expressions of faith.

Building this circle of support hasn't always been easy. It has required vulnerability—being willing to admit needs and struggles. It has demanded time and energy—investing in relationships even when life is busy. It has necessitated wisdom—discerning which relationships are truly supportive versus those that might be draining or harmful.

Yet the effort has been worth it. This circle of support has sustained me through challenges that might otherwise have defeated me. It has provided perspective when my vision became limited. It has offered correction when I started to veer off course. It has celebrated victories that would have been hollow if experienced alone.

THE LEGACY OF RELATIONSHIPS

As I look back on my life and ministry, I'm increasingly aware that relationships are the true legacy we leave. Not buildings or programs or achievements, but the lives we've touched, the people we've influenced, the connections we've nurtured.

"My misery becomes your ministry. The very challenges that could have destroyed you become the means through which you help others. That's how the Master works—taking what seems broken and using it to bring healing."

This perspective has transformed how I view both past pain and present purpose. The relationships I missed in childhood—particularly with my biological father—have informed the relationships I now invest in with young men who need a father figure. The struggles I experienced with learning and education have prepared me to mentor others who face similar challenges.

Nothing is wasted in God's economy.

Every relationship — even difficult or painful ones — shapes us.

Every connection — even brief or seemingly insignificant ones — affects us.

Every interaction—whether positive or negative—teaches us something about ourselves and others.

"Often the things you consider an issue or a challenge is also the very thing God wants to use to change your life, to move you in a new direction and to bless you."

The Master weaves all these relationships together into the tapestry of our lives. He brings people into our path at precisely the right moments. He orchestrates connections that seem random but prove to be pivotal. He uses every relationship —whether lasting decades or just minutes—to shape us for our unique purpose.

As you build your circle, remember that these relationships aren't just about what you receive; they're about what you give. They're not just about who helps you; they're about who you help. They're not just about your growth; they're about the growth you facilitate in others.

"You need people who can speak truth into your life with love—people who don't just point out your weaknesses but help you develop your strengths, who don't just identify problems but help you find solutions, who don't just see you as you are but envision what you can become with God's help."

This is the essence of iron sharpening iron—mutual growth, reciprocal influence, shared transformation. It's about recognizing that we all have something to give and something to receive in every relationship God orchestrates.

PERSONAL REFLECTION

Again a reflection on Proverbs 27:17. It tells us that "iron sharpeneth iron; so a man sharpeneth the countenance of his friend." For years, I understood this primarily as how others made me better — how my mentors challenged me, how my friends supported me, how my community shaped me.

When I mentor young men, I'm not just sharpening them; they're sharpening me. When I build relationships with people from different backgrounds, I'm not just influencing them; they're influencing me. When I pour into others, I'm not just filling their cups; my own cup is being filled in the process.

This mutual sharpening reflects the Master's wisdom in how He designed human connection. He didn't create us to function in isolation or in one-directional relationships. He created us for community—for give and take, for mutual growth, for reciprocal transformation.

Even Jesus, though He was the ultimate teacher and mentor, allowed Himself to be moved by those He encountered. He marveled at the centurion's faith. He was touched by the Syrophoenician woman's persistence. He was affected by His disciples' questions and struggles.

If Jesus Himself experienced the mutual nature of human connection, how much more should we recognize that every relationship God brings into our lives is an opportunity not just to sharpen others but to be sharpened ourselves—to have our own "countenance" changed through the divine gift of iron sharpening iron.

This also lead me to talk about healing. Another aspect of "iron sharpening iron." Healing is so important. Not only healing a wound but healing the heart.

I've learned that healing works best when there's forgiveness. When one looks in the mirror- looking at themselves and not blaming others. Forgiveness is always for you. Which ultimately allows you to heal and walk in the now.

REFLECTION QUESTIONS

1. Who are the people in your life who have "sharpened" you most significantly, and how have they done so?

2. How might your own challenges and struggles uniquely qualify you to mentor or support others?

3. What qualities do you look for in building your circle of supportive relationships?

4. In what ways have you grown through mentoring others or supporting their growth?

5. How might God be using your current relationships to prepare you for future aspects of your calling?

CHAPTER 8:

WALKING IN FAITH

"This year marks the 50th year that I've accepted Christ in my life. It was vacation Bible school June 1975, Pastor Roy I Greer opened the doors of the church and I accepted Jesus Christ as my Lord and Savior."

"For we walk by faith, not by sight." — 2 Corinthians 5:7

THE FOUNDATION OF FAITH

Faith has been the bedrock of my life. Without it, I don't know how I would have navigated the challenges of ADHD, the pain of being labeled, the doors that closed in education and career, the struggles in ministry. Faith provided the foundation that enabled me to stand when everything else seemed to crumble.

I was thirteen years old when I made that decision—old enough to understand what I was doing but young enough that it would shape my entire adolescence and adulthood. That moment at vacation Bible school became an anchor I would return to again and again throughout my life.

My faith wasn't just a product of that moment, though. It had been nurtured by my mother and grandmother, who lived what they believed rather than just talking about it. They didn't just take me to church; they showed me what it meant to trust God through challenges, to pray with expectation, to live with integrity even when it was difficult.

"My mother would always encourage me. I would always talk to my mother about my feelings."

This foundation proved essential as I faced the unique challenges that came with my undiagnosed ADHD. When I struggled in school, my faith reminded me that God had a purpose for me beyond academics. When I failed at college, my faith assured me that my worth wasn't determined by degrees or credentials. When I lost jobs, my faith sustained the hope that God was directing me toward something better.

Faith wasn't just about spiritual comfort—though it certainly provided that. It was practical. It shaped how I approached challenges, how I viewed myself, how I related to others, how I made decisions. It wasn't separate from everyday life; it infused every aspect of it.

FAITH IN THE DARKNESS

There were times when holding onto faith was particularly difficult—dark nights of the soul when God seemed distant and His purposes unclear. Those were the moments when faith was most necessary and most challenging.

"I remember wishing that I could just wake up one morning and I would be really, really smart."

As a child and young adult, I prayed constantly that God would suddenly transform my brain—that I would wake up one day able to read fluently, comprehend quickly, write clearly. I wanted a miraculous intervention that would make me like everyone else. When that miracle didn't come in the way I expected, it tested my faith.

During those dark times, faith wasn't about feeling; it was about choosing. Choosing to believe God had a purpose even when I couldn't see it. Choosing to trust His guidance even when the path seemed to lead nowhere. Choosing to believe in my worth even when circumstances suggested otherwise.

"I still did not feel complete on the inside. I still had questions about my life, but I just didn't know which way to go."

This wrestling with God—this honest struggle to maintain faith amid confusion and pain—became an important part of my spiritual journey. It wasn't just about believing when everything made sense; it was about persevering in faith when nothing seemed to make sense at all.

MASTER'S TOUCH MOMENT

After I lost my job at MTA, I was sitting alone in my living room, overwhelmed with questions and doubts. I opened my Bible randomly, seeking some word of comfort or direction. My eyes fell on Jeremiah 29:11: "For I know the thoughts that I think toward you, saith the LORD, thoughts of peace, and not of evil, to give you an expected end." In that moment, I felt God's presence so strongly that tears flowed down my face. The Master was showing me that even this painful transition was part of His plan—a plan for my good, not my harm.

FAITH AND UNDERSTANDING

My ADHD diagnosis at age 37 transformed not just my understanding of myself but also my understanding of faith. It helped me see that God's work in my life wasn't about changing my brain to be like everyone else's; it was about using my unique brain for purposes only I could fulfill.

This revelation was profoundly spiritual. It wasn't just a clinical diagnosis; it was a reframing of my entire life through the lens of divine purpose. It wasn't just about a neurological difference; it was about God's intentional design. It wasn't just about accommodating a limitation; it was about embracing a unique calling.

"So getting diagnosed with ADHD, just opened my world up. And it began to help me to understand who I was. It helped me to understand more through therapy. We were able to talk about my childhood, my teen years, my young adult years. The trauma of not making it through Hurley, not making it through college.I learned that I was uniquely different, and that I learned differently, and ultimately that I was okay just the way <u>I was,</u> -an d

the way I <u>was NOT.</u> "

This integration of faith and understanding became central to my ministry. I began to see that what I had experienced wasn't just for me; it was for others who felt labeled and limited, who struggled to see God's purpose in their challenges, who needed to know they were designed intentionally even if differently.

"It has not been an easy run. Life is full of ups and downs. My faith is really what has helped me and what has brought me to where I am today."

Faith provided the framework for making sense of my life—not just intellectually understanding it but finding meaning and purpose in it. It allowed me to see divine intention where others might see only limitation or dysfunction. It enabled me to recognize the Master's touch in every aspect of my journey.

FAITH IN ACTION

Throughout my life, faith has never been merely theoretical. It has been practical, actionable, lived out in daily choices and commitments. It has shaped how I've approached work, relationships, ministry, challenges — every aspect of my life.

This strong sense of self was rooted in my faith — in the belief that God had created me with purpose and value regardless of what others might say or think. It gave me the courage to resist negative influences, to maintain integrity even when it was difficult, to pursue my calling despite obstacles.

My faith also shaped my approach to work. I didn't just work to earn money; I worked as an expression of spiritual values — integrity, excellence, service, dignity.

Even working as a janitor at Mount Olive Baptist Church for over 30 years became a spiritual discipline — a way of serving God and His people with excellence regardless of the task's prestige or visibility. It was faith in action, not just faith in concept.

My approach to relationships was similarly shaped by faith. I tried to see others as God saw them — with inherent value and potential regardless of their background or circumstances. This perspective was especially important in my jail ministry, where I encountered men whom society had written off but whom God still loved and had purposes for.

In all these areas — work, relationships, ministry — faith wasn't separate from action. It was the motivation for action, the guide for action, the purpose behind action. It made the ordinary sacred and the mundane meaningful.

FAITH THROUGH TESTING

Any faith worth having will be tested. Mine certainly has been. Through educational struggles, job losses, health challenges, ministry difficulties, and personal disappointments, my faith has faced trials that either could have destroyed it or deepened it.

"I believe that God knew I would be this way. And I believe that my life was designed this way. The course has been preplanned, and I'm where I'm supposed to be."

This perspective didn't come easily or automatically. It developed through wrestling with difficult questions, through honest conversations with God, through periods of doubt and confusion. It emerged as I learned to see God's purposes even in painful experiences.

One significant test came when I left Mount Olive Baptist Church after decades of membership and service. This was the church where I had been baptized and where I had been licensed to preach. I not only served as a part time janitor for over 30 years; there was much more. My service included Sunday School teaching, President of the User Board, and walked closely with Pastor Greer.

After the death of Pastor Greer, Pastor Major Stewart became the new Pastor of Mount Olive Baptist Church in November of 2009. After 4.5 years, I felt it was time to leave to expand to the next level of ministry. Leaving was painful and disorienting.

This was a profound test of faith. Not just faith in God but faith in His church, His people, His process of working through community. It would have been easy to become bitter, to reject organized religion, to withdraw from ministry altogether.

Instead, this test ultimately deepened my faith. It helped me distinguish between faith in God and faith in particular expressions or communities of faith. It forced me to rely more directly on God rather than on familiar structures and relationships. It prepared me for the next chapter of ministry that would come later at Hill Road Baptist Church.

MASTER'S TOUCH MOMENT

During my first Sunday at a new church in Grand Rapids after leaving Mount Olive, I felt out of place and still deeply hurt. As worship began, I struggled to engage, my mind still dwelling on the past. Then the congregation began singing a hymn my grandmother had loved. *As the familiar melody washed over me, I felt her presence and remembered her unwavering faith through much greater challenges than I was facing.* In that moment, the Master touched me through memory and music, reminding me that faith is a legacy that transcends individual churches or experiences.

FAITH AND SCRIPTURE

Scripture has been the anchor for my faith—providing guidance, comfort, challenge, and perspective throughout my journey. Despite the challenges ADHD presented with reading, certain passages became so deeply embedded in my heart and mind that they shaped my entire outlook on life.

"Jeremiah chapter 1 verse 4 and 5 says, 'Then the word of the Lord came unto me, saying, Before I formed thee in the belly I knew thee; and before thou camest forth out of the womb I sanctified thee, and I ordained thee a prophet unto the nations.'"

This verse transformed how I viewed my birth as a premature baby who wasn't breathing. It wasn't random; it was part of God's intentional design. He knew me before I was formed. He had purposes for me before I took my first breath.

"Philippians 4-13 says, 'I can do all things through Christ who strengthens me.' I just want you to know, my sisters, my brothers, no matter your age, or no matter your color, you can do it today."

This verse became my mantra when facing challenges that seemed insurmountable. It wasn't about my abilities but about Christ's strength working through me. It wasn't a guarantee that everything would be easy but a promise that I wouldn't face anything alone.

"Romans 8-28 says, 'And we know that all things work together for the good to them that love God, to them who are the called according to his purpose.'"

When I struggled to understand why certain doors closed or why particular challenges persisted, this verse provided perspective. It assured me that nothing was wasted, that every experience — even painful ones — was being woven into a larger purpose.

"Romans 8 verse 31: 'What shall we then say to these things? If God be for us, who can be against us?' God gave me this scripture February 8, 1993, and it was my 31st birthday."

This verse became particularly meaningful as I faced opposition or doubt from others. It reminded me that God's opinion of me mattered more than human judgments, that His purposes for me would prevail despite obstacles.

These scriptures weren't just nice sayings or motivational quotes. They were lifelines during dark times, correctives when my perspective became distorted, guides when the path forward wasn't clear. They formed the foundation of both my personal faith and my public ministry.

FAITH AS SURRENDER

Perhaps the most challenging aspect of faith has been learning to surrender—to release my own plans, preferences, and expectations in favor of God's purposes. This hasn't come naturally or easily. It has been a lifelong process of gradually opening my hands and releasing my grip on how I think my life should be.

"You can't be afraid to ask questions. You can't be afraid to say " Hey! I don't understand, can you help me?" You have to be able to speak, and you have to have strong people around you."

Surrender didn't mean passivity. It didn't mean sitting back and waiting for God to magically transform my circumstances. It meant actively seeking help, pursuing growth, using the resources and relationships God provided. But it also meant recognizing that ultimately, the outcomes were in His hands, not mine.

"Reading is not something that I like. I've learned to read more and more as I continue to grow older. I read better now. I read more now than I ever have in my life."

Surrender meant accepting my limitations while still working to grow beyond them. It meant acknowledging that I might never read with the ease or speed others did but continuing to improve rather than giving up. It meant working with my design rather than against it.

"I have learned that no one person knows everything."

This simple but profound realization was part of my surrender — acknowledging that I didn't have to know everything or be capable of everything. I could rely on others for help in areas where I struggled. I could contribute my unique gifts while accepting assistance in areas of weakness.

"ADHD is no joke. No, I don't drink. I don't smoke. I don't get high, but I have certainly hurt myself pretty much all of my adult life. Not feeling good, not measuring up, not feeling like I am normal."

The most difficult surrender was releasing the self-criticism and shame I had carried for so long. Accepting that I was exactly as God intended me to be — not deficient or defective but uniquely designed for specific purposes. This surrender required not just releasing my own expectations but also letting go of the labels and limitations others had placed on me.

This is the paradox of faith as surrender: In releasing our grip on how we think our lives should be, we open ourselves to how they were meant to be. In surrendering our limited vision, we embrace God's expansive one. In letting go of our small dreams, we make room for His larger purposes.

FAITH FOR THE JOURNEY AHEAD

At over 60 years old, I continue to walk by faith. The journey isn't over. There are still challenges to face, growth to experience, ministry to fulfill. Faith remains the foundation for whatever lies ahead.

Hebrews 11:1 (King James Version) says:

"Now faith is the substance of things hoped for, the evidence of things not seen." Hebrews 11:6 (King James Version) says:

"But without faith it is impossible to please him: for he that cometh to God must believe that he is, and that he is a rewarder of them that diligently seek him."

"I believe I have some things to do in this life before I leave this earth. I believe I have some more assignments. I believe I have more preaching opportunities. I believe that I have more speaking opportunities. I believe that I have to write this book, and I believe that I'm going to make it."

This faith isn't blind optimism. It's rooted in experience—in seeing how God has worked through every aspect of my journey so far, how He has used even the most painful or challenging circumstances for good, how He has revealed His purposes in unexpected ways.

"ADHD is a GIFT for my life. I've met some wonderful people who have assisted me in my life. They make the difference."

What I once saw as a curse, I now recognize as a gift—not despite my faith but because of it. Faith has given me the perspective to see divine design where others might see only disorder, to recognize blessing where others might see only burden, to discern purpose where others might see only problem.

"I continue to look at my life from the time I was conceived to this very moment 60+ years later. You are given a diagnosis, but you have to know that you're bigger than whatever the diagnosis is."

This is the essence of walking by faith, not by sight. It's seeing beyond what is immediately visible to what God is accomplishing beneath the surface. It's recognizing the Master's touch even when circumstances seem random or chaotic. It's trusting the divine hand guiding the journey even when the path seems unclear.

"My faith in God and what my mother, my grandmother, my sister have instilled in me, has helped me to be the man that I am today."

Faith doesn't eliminate challenges. It doesn't guarantee ease or comfort or conventional success. But it provides the framework for finding meaning in challenges, the strength for facing them with courage, the perspective for seeing them as preparation rather than punishment.

As I look toward whatever time remains in my journey, faith continues to be my guide and strength. Not a rigid, simplistic faith that denies difficulties, but a robust, tested faith that has been forged through them. Not a faith that eliminates questions, but one that provides anchor points amid uncertainty. Not a faith that removes obstacles, but one that reveals their purpose.

This is my testimony and my encouragement to you: Whatever labels have been placed on you, whatever limitations you face, whatever challenges seem insurmountable—the Master who has touched my life can touch yours too. His purposes for you transcend others' perceptions. His design for you encompasses even what seems like a disadvantage. His touch transforms what others discard into what He treasures.

Walk by faith, not by sight. The view is better, even when the path is harder.

PERSONAL REFLECTION

"For we walk by faith, not by sight" (2 Corinthians 5:7) has taken on deeper meaning throughout my journey. When I first encountered this verse as a young believer, I thought it simply meant believing in God despite not being able to see Him physically.

But life with ADHD has taught me a more profound interpretation. Walking by faith means trusting God's design when society sees only disorder. It means believing in divine purpose when educational systems see only deficiency. It means recognizing the Master's touch even when others see only limitations.

Walking by faith, not by sight, means seeing beyond the immediate and visible — beyond the diagnoses, the labels, the closed doors, the failed attempts. It means looking past what appears to be true according to worldly standards to what is eternally true according to God's perspective.

When I couldn't see the purpose in my life, faith allowed me to trust there was one. When I couldn't see the reason for my learning struggles, faith assured me they were preparing me for unique ministry. When I couldn't see why certain doors closed, faith helped me trust that better ones would open.

This kind of faith isn't blind; it's visionary. It doesn't ignore reality; it perceives a deeper reality. It doesn't deny challenges; it discovers their purpose. Walking by faith means living with the conviction that God's invisible purposes are more real and enduring than the visible obstacles that seem to define our lives.

REFLECTION QUESTIONS

1. How has faith helped you navigate challenges or limitations in your life?

2. What scripture verses have become anchors for you during difficult times?

3. Where might God be asking you to surrender your own plans or expectations in favor of His purposes?

4. How have you experienced God's guidance when the path forward wasn't clear?

5. What limitations or challenges in your life might actually be part of God's unique design and calling for you?

CHAPTER 9:

YOUR UNIQUE DESIGN

"I had to learn that I must appreciate who I am. I believe that God knew I would be this way. And I believe that my life was designed this way."

> *"I will praise thee; for I am fearfully and wonderfully made: marvelous are thy works; and that my soul knoweth right well."* — Psalm 139:14

CREATED WITH PURPOSE

From the moment I discovered I was born stillborn—a four-pound premature baby who wasn't breathing—I began to see my life differently. What seemed like a tragic beginning revealed something profound: the Master had touched me before I took my first breath. What appeared to be a disadvantage was actually part of a divine design.

This scripture transformed my view of myself and my challenges. It wasn't just inspirational platitude; it was a divine declaration about my design. It wasn't a mistake. My ADHD wasn't an accident. My learning differences weren't defects. I was "fearfully and wonderfully made" exactly as God intended me to be.

"In reading this scripture Psalm 139:14, it lets me know that God already had me in his mind. Jesus had a plan, a purpose, and an assignment that I, - and only I, can do; regardless of the diagnosis, regardless of people's perception of me, regardless of how I was feeling or thinking about myself."

The revelation that God designed me—with my specific brain wiring, with my particular strengths and challenges, with my unique way of processing information — changed everything. It shifted my focus from what I couldn't do to what only I could do.

This understanding didn't come quickly or easily. It emerged gradually through therapy, through scripture study, through ministry experiences, through relationships with people who saw my potential rather than just my limitations. It developed as I began to recognize patterns in my life that pointed to purpose rather than just coincidence.

Understanding your unique design begins with acceptance—not resignation to limitation but recognition of divine intention. It begins with the belief that God doesn't make mistakes, that your differences aren't defects but distinctions that equip you for your specific calling and purpose.

DISCOVERING YOUR DESIGN

My journey to discovering my unique design took decades. For most of my life, I tried to be like everyone else, to overcome what I saw as deficiencies, to succeed by conventional standards despite my challenges.

"I would go to school every day, and I just didn't understand the classwork. I did not understand Math. I was not able to spell words properly."

"I'm a visual learner. I can watch you. However, in watching you, I can pick it up."

Through therapy and self-discovery, I began to identify patterns in how I functioned best. I realized that while reading, writing, and traditional learning were difficult for me, I excelled at visual learning, at connecting with people, at practical problem-solving, at speaking and teaching when I could do so in my own way.

"I now know that I am a man of consistency. I've also learned that I work best when things are in order."

This self-awareness became crucial. I discovered that I needed order and structure to function optimally. I learned that consistency in relationships and routines helped me navigate a world that wasn't designed for how my brain worked. I found that technology could bridge gaps between my challenges and my capabilities.

MASTER'S TOUCH MOMENT

During a conversation with a young man I was mentoring, I was explaining a biblical concept in my usual animated way—using gestures, varying my tone, painting word pictures. He interrupted me to say, "Pastor Kenneth, you explain things differently than anyone I've ever heard, but I understand it better." In that moment, I realized the Master had designed even my communication style to reach people conventional teaching might miss. What others might see as an unpolished presentation was actually a uniquely effective approach for certain listeners.

Discovering your unique design requires honest self-assessment. It means identifying not just your challenges but also your strengths. It involves recognizing patterns in what energizes you versus what drains you, what comes naturally versus what requires extraordinary effort, what yields fruit versus what produces frustration.

As you discover your design, confidence grows. Not arrogance or pretense, but genuine confidence in who God made you to be and what He's equipped you to do. This confidence doesn't deny challenges but faces them with the assurance that you have what you need to overcome them or work around them.

EMBRACING YOUR DISTINCTIONS

Once I began to understand my unique design, the next step was embracing it— not just accepting it intellectually but actively engaging with it, operating from it, celebrating it rather than compensating for it.

This perspective represented a complete reversal from how I had viewed my condition for most of my life. What I had seen as a curse, I now recognized as a gift. What I had experienced as a limitation, I now understood as a distinction that qualified me for unique purposes.

"I love spending time with seniors, older women, older men. I love talking to seniors about their life, their wisdom, their knowledge, their experiences."

This natural connection with seniors became one of my distinctions. While many younger ministers focused on youth or young adults, I found I had a gift for relating to older individuals—hearing their stories, valuing their wisdom, honoring their experiences. This wasn't random; it was part of my design, shaped by being raised by an older mother and grandmother.

"I learned that I was a good driver. And so I started developing and driving. That job built me."

Driving became another distinction. When I discovered I was a good driver, it opened doors to various opportunities—from MTA bus driving - to the
transportation ministry at church - and then two years at a limousine service from 2007-2009. What might seem like an ordinary skill became a significant component of my calling and service.

Even my attention to vehicle maintenance and appearance became a distinction — reflecting my visual learning style, my need for order, and my belief that excellence in small things prepares you for excellence in greater responsibilities. What might seem trivial to some became an expression of my values and character.

MASTER'S TOUCH MOMENT

When I was in my forties, I was asked to speak at a senior citizens' event. I was nervous because many in attendance were retired educators and professionals. As I spoke, I noticed an elderly woman in the front row nodding and smiling. Afterward, she approached me and said, "Young man, do you know why I connected with your message? Because you speak with your whole self—not just your words, but your expressions, your gestures, your energy. My grandson has what they call ADHD, and he communicates just like you." What I had worried might be a liability —my animated, sometimes non-linear communication style—was actually a divinely designed connection point with both her and her grandson.

Embracing your distinctions means recognizing that what sets you apart doesn't separate you from purpose; it prepares you for it. It means seeing how your unique combination of strengths, challenges, experiences, and perspective qualifies you for contributions others might not be able to make.

The very areas where I struggled — reading, writing, traditional academics — pushed me to develop other strengths. My difficulty with written communication enhanced my oral communication. My struggles with traditional education deepened my empathy for others who didn't fit conventional molds.

Embracing your distinctions isn't just about recognizing strengths that compensate for challenges. It's about seeing how even the challenges themselves can be transformed into qualifications for unique service and purpose.

DESIGNED FOR CONNECTION

One of the most significant aspects of my unique design has been its orientation toward people. Despite — or perhaps because of—my challenges with traditional learning, I developed a natural ability to connect with others, to understand their needs, to communicate in ways that resonated with them.

"I enjoy people. I enjoy helping people. I enjoy learning."

This wasn't just a preference; it was core to my design. Where I struggled with textbooks and written instructions, I thrived with people and experiential learning. Where conventional education often failed me, relationships consistently nurtured and developed me.

My ability to build relationships became one of my greatest assets. Throughout my life, connections with people opened doors that might otherwise have remained closed due to my learning challenges. People who knew me personally looked beyond my limitations to see my character, work ethic, and potential.

This relational orientation became particularly important in ministry. While I might struggle more than other ministers with the academic aspects of sermon preparation or biblical exegesis, I excelled at connecting with people in ways that made the message accessible and impactful.

As I embraced this aspect of my design, I stopped trying to be the kind of minister who impresses with scholarly knowledge or eloquent oration. Instead, I focused on being authentic, on making complex concepts understandable, on relating scripture to real-life experiences in ways people could apply practically.

"The Master's touch kept me humble because I knew that it wasn't me. It was the touch of God that touched me to then go and touch the heart of these young men."

This humility became essential. Recognizing that my effectiveness came not from my own abilities but from God working through my unique design kept me dependent on Him rather than confident in myself. It maintained the awareness that whatever impact I had was the result of the Master's touch, not my own talent or effort.

DESIGNED FOR COMPASSION

Another significant element of my design has been a deep capacity for compassion — particularly for those who, like me, have been labeled, limited, or misunderstood by others.

"I saw the man's heart. And that's key. Not the clothes that they wear. Not the crime that they committed. But I saw their hearts."

This ability to see beyond external circumstances to the heart within became central to my jail ministry. Where others might see only criminals, offenders, inmates, I saw men with stories, with pain, with potential, with divine design of their own.

My experience with being "different" prepared me uniquely for crossing cultural and racial boundaries. Having been labeled and limited because of my learning differences, I had developed sensitivity to being defined by external characteristics rather than internal character. This gave me insight and compassion that helped bridge divides others might find difficult to cross.

"One thing that I have learned about my ADHD talking with my Aunt Annie... It takes me a while to read. It takes me a while to comprehend. But when I get it, I get it, and I get it for life."

My own struggles with learning created patience with others who learn differently or who need more time to grasp concepts. Rather than becoming frustrated with those who don't understand quickly, I can relate to their experience and walk alongside them with genuine empathy.

This compassion isn't just a nice quality; it's an essential component of my calling and effectiveness. It's not separate from my ADHD;

it's directly connected to it. What might be seen as a deficit in some contexts becomes an asset in ministry contexts where understanding, patience, and genuine caring matter more than efficiency or conventional expertise.

DESIGNED FOR RESILIENCE

Perhaps the most important aspect of my design has been resilience — the capacity to persist despite setbacks, to keep moving forward despite obstacles, to maintain hope despite disappointments.

"My mother always encouraged me. You can do it, you can do it. Now my childhood years were challenging. My teenage years were challenging. Being in special ed was something that I really didn't understand. I just never felt like I was normal like the other kids."

This encouragement from my mother laid the foundation for resilience. Her constant affirmation — "You can do it" — became an internal voice that countered the external voices telling me I couldn't, I wouldn't, I shouldn't even try.

"I lost a job at 20 years old because I didn't have the grade point average they required. So that was the beginning of the journey, but not knowing what it was."

Each setback tested this resilience. Each closed door, each failed attempt at education, each job loss challenged the belief that I could "do it." Yet somehow, through my mother's encouragement, through community support, through faith, through the Master's touch, I kept moving forward.

"I can't be who everybody wants me to be, but I can be me. And that was also instilled in my home. Be Kenneth Rommel Gillard. Pastor Greer was always telling me "Be yourself". But it's a struggle because people don't want you to be you. People want you to be what they want you to be."

This insistence on authenticity — on being who God designed me to be rather than who others wanted me to be — became crucial to resilience. It provided an anchor amid pressures to conform, to deny my challenges, to present myself as something I wasn't.

"You have to know that you're bigger and better than the diagnosis. You have to be

strong. You have to persevere, you to continue to push forward in your life."

Resilience doesn't mean denying challenges; it means facing them with determination. It doesn't mean pretending limitations don't exist; it means refusing to be defined by them. It doesn't mean never falling; it means getting back up every time you do.

DESIGNED FOR THIS TIME

As I've come to understand and embrace my unique design, I've also recognized that it isn't just about me — it's about the contribution I'm designed to make, the people I'm designed to reach, the purpose I'm designed to fulfill in this specific time and context.

"You have to look inward and that's a hard thing to do, but you got to go with what's on the inside. You got to go with you."

This inward journey — discovering who you truly are and what you're uniquely designed to contribute — isn't selfish; it's strategic. It's not about self-focus but about discerning divine design so you can fulfill your purpose effectively.

What seemed like rejection in that moment — being moved from the regular classroom to special education — was actually direction. It was the beginning of a journey that would eventually lead to ministry uniquely suited to those who feel different, labeled, limited, or marginalized.

"You have to have a mindset to work in those systems. Certainly as a Pastor, preacher, a minister, a volunteer. When you go in, I would encourage any person that wants to do this type of work, that you go in with an open heart and mind and know that it's not you that's doing the work. It's God in you."

This understanding—that God works through our unique design rather than despite it—has been transformative. It has shifted my perspective from trying to overcome my differences to embracing them as essential to my calling and effectiveness.

Even difficult transitions — like leaving Mount Olive after decades — have been part of the design. What seemed like an ending opened the door to new relationships, new ministry opportunities, new growth that wouldn't have been possible without that painful transition.

Divine design includes not just our abilities and challenges but also our timing — when certain doors open or close, when particular relationships form or end, when specific opportunities arise or disappear. All of it works together to position us exactly where we need to be for our unique contribution.

HELPING OTHERS DISCOVER THEIR DESIGN

As I've come to understand and embrace my own unique design, I've become passionate about helping others discover theirs — especially those who, like me, may not fit conventional molds or meet traditional expectations.

"You need to look deep, deep within, and you gotta surround yourself with good people, people that speak well in your life, people that will encourage you, people that may not always speak the way you want them to speak about you, but they are honest, they're truthful, they're loving, and they believe the best for you, and your life."

This process requires both internal reflection and external support. It involves honest self-assessment but also relationships with people who can see what you might miss about yourself, who can speak truth with love, who can recognize potential you may not yet perceive.

"Nobody made me go to therapy for eight years. I went because I wanted to know who I was."

Therapy played a crucial role in my journey to self-understanding. Having a trained professional help me unpack my experiences, recognize patterns, understand my brain wiring, and process the emotions connected to my challenges was invaluable. Not everyone will need eight years of therapy, but most of us need some form of guided self-discovery.

Understanding your design is a process, not an event. It unfolds over time, through various experiences, relationships, challenges, and opportunities. It involves not just recognizing your wiring but also learning how to work with it, how to navigate a world that might not accommodate it, how to fulfill your purpose through it rather than despite it.

"I'm sharing these things with you for you to know that you can do it too. You can achieve. You must remember you're not like anyone else. God only made you."

This has become my message to others — that their unique design isn't a mistake but intentional, that their differences aren't defects but distinctions, that their challenges don't disqualify them from purpose but may actually be essential to it.

Whether through preaching, counseling, mentoring, or casual conversation, I try to help others see themselves through God's eyes rather than through the limiting labels others have placed on them. I share my own journey not as a template for theirs but as evidence that the Master's touch can transform what seems like limitation into qualification for a unique purpose.

PERSONAL REFLECTION

Psalm 139:14 declares, "I will praise thee; for I am fearfully and wonderfully made: marvellous are thy works; and that my soul knoweth right well." For most of my life, I struggled to believe this applied to me. I saw others as "wonderfully made" while viewing myself as somehow deficient, flawed, less than.

My journey with ADHD has taught me the profound truth of this scripture. Being "fearfully and wonderfully made" doesn't mean being made like everyone else. It doesn't mean being without challenges or differences. It means being uniquely designed by a Creator who doesn't mass-produce but crafts each person with intention and purpose.

When the psalmist says, "that my soul knoweth right well," he points to an inner knowing—a deep recognition of divine design that transcends external appearances or conventional standards. This knowing doesn't come easily or automatically. For me, it emerged gradually through therapy, through ministry experiences, through relationships with people who saw my value, through moments when my unique design proved perfectly suited for particular purposes.

I now understand that being "fearfully and wonderfully made" includes my ADHD, my learning differences, my visual processing, my communication style — all of it. None of it is accidental. None of it is defective. All of it is part of a divine design that qualifies me for a unique contribution that someone wired differently couldn't make in quite the same way.

The marvelous work isn't just my physical body but my entire being — including the brain that processes information differently, the heart that connects deeply with others' pain, the spirit that perseveres despite challenges. Every aspect of how I'm made reveals the Master's touch— intentional, purposeful, wonderfully suited for the calling only I can fulfill.

REFLECTION QUESTIONS

1. What unique aspects of your design — whether strengths, challenges, or differences — might be preparing you for a specific purpose?

2. Who are the people in your life who see beyond your limitations to recognize your unique potential?

3. What patterns have you noticed in when you feel most alive, effective, or purposeful? How

might these point to aspects of your divine design?

4. In what ways have your challenges actually equipped you for particular opportunities or relationships?

5. How might embracing rather than fighting against your unique design change your approach to current difficulties or decisions?

CHAPTER 10:

YOUR EXPECTED END

"God has been good to me from the beginning of time."

> *"For I know the thoughts that I think toward you, saith the LORD, thoughts of peace, and not of evil, to give you an expected end."* — Jeremiah 29:11

THE JOURNEY'S PURPOSE

As I reflect on my journey—from being born stillborn to struggling through school to discovering my ADHD diagnosis at age 37 to finding purpose in ministry — I'm struck by the pattern that emerges. What once appeared random now reveals divine intention. What seemed like limitation now shows itself as preparation. What looked like detour now proves to have been direction all along.

"For I know the thoughts that I think toward you, saith the LORD, thoughts of peace, and not of evil, to give you an expected end."

This promise from Jeremiah 29:11 has become more meaningful to me with each passing year. God's thoughts toward me haven't been thoughts of punishment or restriction but thoughts of peace—of wholeness, purpose, and fulfillment. Even the most painful experiences, the most challenging limitations, the most disappointing setbacks were being woven into a tapestry of purpose I couldn't yet see.

This isn't just positive thinking. It's recognition of the Master's touch throughout every aspect of my life — beginning quite literally with that first touch that started my breathing after being born stillborn. It's acknowledgment that even what seemed like disadvantage was actually divine design for specific purpose.

"I know that I'm a gift. I know that I was given to mankind by God. I was given the ability to touch many lives."

This understanding gives meaning to the struggle. It provides purpose for the pain. It offers direction for the journey ahead. It assures me that the Master who has guided every step thus far will continue to guide every step to come.

As you consider your own journey — with whatever challenges, limitations, or differences you face — I hope you'll recognize the same pattern. The Master's touch isn't just in dramatic moments of intervention; it's in the daily unfolding of your life, the gradual revelation of your purpose, the unexpected ways your unique design qualifies you for contribution only you can make.

THE FIVE STEPS REVISITED

Throughout this book, I've shared my journey of overcoming labels and limitations. In Chapter 5, I outlined five steps that helped me move from being defined by limitations to discovering my unique purpose. As we conclude, I want to revisit these steps as a framework for your own journey forward.

Step One: Accept Your Difference

Acceptance doesn't mean resignation to limitation; it means recognition of unique design. It means understanding that your differences aren't defects but distinctions that qualify you for specific purposes. It means acknowledging challenges honestly while refusing to be defined by them.

For me, accepting my ADHD and learning differences was the foundation for everything that followed. Without this acceptance, I would have continued trying to be someone I wasn't designed to be, striving for success in ways that didn't align with how God wired me, missing the unique contribution only I could make.

Step Two: Seek Help

No one overcomes significant challenges alone. We need others who can provide support, perspective, tools, and guidance. For me, eight years of therapy with Dr. Bates was crucial. For you, it might be counseling, coaching, mentoring, support groups, or other resources.

Seeking help isn't weakness; it's wisdom. It's recognition that we're designed for community, that we need each other's gifts and perspectives, that no one person has all the answers or resources. It's humility to acknowledge needs and courage to reach out for assistance.

Step Three: Stop Comparing

Comparison is the thief of joy and purpose. When we measure ourselves against others — their achievements, their abilities, their apparent ease in areas where we struggle — we diminish our own unique value and contribution.

Stopping comparison doesn't mean stopping growth. I still work to improve my reading, my comprehension, my communication. But I do so on my own terms, at my own pace, for my own purposes — not in competition with others or in pursuit of their validation.

Step Four: Surround Yourself with Supporters

The people around you will either lift you toward your potential or limit you to their perceptions. Choose wisely. Surround yourself with those who see beyond your challenges to your capacity, who speak truth with love, who believe in your purpose even when you doubt it yourself.

For me, this circle began with my mother's constant encouragement — "You can do it, Kenny" — and expanded to include mentors like Pastor Greer and Pastor Dantzler, therapists like Dr. Bates, peers who saw my value, and eventually those I mentored who reflected back to me the impact of my life and ministry.

Step Five: Forgive and Be Grateful

Forgiveness — of yourself and others — frees you to move forward rather than remaining stuck in past pain or resentment. Gratitude transforms even difficult experiences from burdens into blessings, from obstacles into opportunities, from limitations into qualifications for unique purposes.

For me, forgiving those who had labeled and limited me — teachers, employers, sometimes even friends and family — was essential to my healing and growth. Equally important was forgiving myself for the years I believed those labels and limitations defined me. And beyond forgiveness, developing gratitude for even the challenges has allowed me to see divine purpose in every aspect of my journey.

MASTER'S TOUCH MOMENT

On my 60th birthday, a young man I had mentored through his own learning challenges brought me a gift — a journal with Jeremiah 29:11 inscribed on the cover. Inside, he had written a note: "Pastor Kenneth, your life shows me that God's 'expected end' isn't about becoming like everyone else but becoming exactly who He designed you to be. Thank you for teaching me that my challenges aren't punishments but preparation." That moment crystallized for me the purpose of all my struggles — not just what they produced in me but what they allowed me to offer others facing similar journeys.

These five steps aren't a formula or a quick fix. They're a framework for an ongoing journey — one that requires persistence, courage, faith, and community. They're a path toward discovering and embracing your unique design, toward recognizing the Master's touch in every aspect of your life, toward fulfilling the purpose for which you were created.

THE MINISTRY OF DIFFERENCE

My experiences with ADHD and learning differences have shaped not just who I am but the ministry I've been called to fulfill. They've given me particular sensitivity to those who feel labeled, limited, marginalized, or misunderstood. They've equipped me to speak authentically about overcoming obstacles and discovering purpose beyond conventional definitions of success.

In the jail ministry especially, my own experience with being labeled allowed me to see beyond inmates' orange jumpsuits to the hearts within. Having felt the pain of being defined by limitations rather than potential, I could recognize and respond to that same pain in men society had written off.

"My misery becomes my ministry. The very challenges that could have destroyed me become the means through which I can help others. That's how the Master works — taking what seems broken and using it to bring healing."

This principle extends beyond formal ministry roles. Whatever challenges you've faced — whether learning differences, physical limitations, mental health struggles, relational wounds, or other difficulties—can become channels through which you offer unique understanding and assistance to others facing similar journeys.

"What I am saying or what I'm trying to say, it has not been an easy run. Life is full of ups and downs. My faith is really what has helped me and what has brought me to where I am today."

In Genesis 50:20, Joseph, addressing his brothers, states, "As for you, you meant evil against me, but God meant it for good, to bring about the present result — the survival of many people".

"We were not put on this earth to be by ourselves. I believe we are put on this earth to build relationships with one another. Connect, love one another, build one another, encourage one another."

This perspective makes every relationship an opportunity for ministry — for mutual encouragement, for sharing wisdom gained through struggle, for reflecting to others their value and potential beyond whatever limitations they face. It transforms how we see not just ourselves but everyone we encounter.

MASTER'S TOUCH MOMENT

After speaking at a men's conference about my journey with ADHD, a father approached me with tears in his eyes. "My son has been diagnosed with ADHD," he said, "and I've been so worried about his future. Hearing your story gives me hope." As we talked, I realized the Master had orchestrated this moment decades earlier—when I was that struggling child, when I was questioning my worth and purpose, when I was praying to wake up "normal." My challenges weren't just preparation for my ministry; they were preparation for this specific conversation with this specific father on this specific day.

The ministry of difference isn't always formal or public. Often it happens in quiet conversations, in one-on-one relationships, in seemingly small moments that prove pivotal for someone struggling to see their value or purpose. It happens when your unique journey enables you to say exactly what someone else needs to hear, to offer precisely the perspective they need to move forward.

"I love my pastor...I loved the people, most of all. I loved God."

This love—for God and for people—is the foundation of the ministry of difference. It's not about techniques or strategies; it's about genuine care that flows from having experienced both struggle and grace, both limitation and liberation, both the pain of being misunderstood and the joy of being truly seen.

THE EXPECTED END

Jeremiah 29:11 speaks of an "expected end" — a purpose and destination God has in mind that provides context and meaning for the journey. This doesn't mean every detail of our lives is predetermined, but it does mean there's divine intention behind our unique design, divine purpose in our specific challenges, divine direction in our particular paths.

The expected end isn't about arriving at some final destination where all challenges disappear.

It's about becoming fully who you're designed to be, fulfilling the purpose for which you're uniquely qualified, offering the contribution only you can make.

This continuing sense of purpose keeps me moving forward even at over 60 years old. The journey isn't over. The Master's touch continues to guide and shape me. The expected end unfolds day by day, relationship by relationship, opportunity by opportunity.

Even seemingly small aspects of life—like how I maintain my vehicles — reflect the influence of those who shaped me, the values they instilled, the standards they modeled. The expected end isn't just about major achievements or formal ministry; it's about how we live each day, how we approach every responsibility, how we honor those who have invested in us.

"I believe with everything within me that I would not be the man I am today if I not had not had the masters touch."

This conviction drives everything — my perspective on the past, my engagement with the present, my vision for the future. The Master's touch has been evident in every aspect of my journey, from that first breath after being born stillborn to the ministry opportunities still unfolding. It will continue until the expected end is fully realized.

YOUR JOURNEY FORWARD

As you reflect on your own journey — with whatever challenges, limitations, or differences you face — I hope you'll recognize the same divine pattern. The Master's touch isn't reserved for those who fit conventional molds or meet traditional expectations. It's for everyone willing to trust that their unique design serves divine purpose, that their specific challenges prepare them for particular contributions, that their individual journey leads to purpose only they can fulfill.

The journey isn't easy. It requires persistence, courage, honesty, and support. It involves setbacks and struggles, questions and doubts, moments of both clarity and confusion. But it's worth every effort, every tear, every challenge overcome.

"You can do it. I can do it. I can get this. I'm gonna make it."

This simple affirmation — first spoken by my mother and now central to my message to others — captures the essence of moving forward with hope and determination. It's not a guarantee that everything will be easy or that every goal will be achieved exactly as envisioned. It's confidence that with God's help, with proper support, with persistent effort, you can fulfill the purpose for which you're uniquely designed.

"You have to know that you're bigger and better than the diagnosis. You have to be strong. You have to persevere. You have to continue to push forward in this life."

Whatever labels have been placed on you — by others or by yourself — they don't define you. Whatever limitations you face — whether physical, mental, emotional, relational, or circumstantial — they don't determine your destiny. Whatever challenges have marked your journey so far, they're preparation rather than punishment, qualification rather than disqualification, direction rather than detour. **"When I look at my life through eyes of gratitude, I don't see a series of limitations and failures—I see a masterfully crafted journey leading me exactly where I needed to be."**

This perspective transforms everything. It doesn't deny difficulties or pretend challenges don't hurt. It doesn't suggest that discrimination or injustice should be accepted or ignored. But it does place everything within a larger context of divine purpose and direction — a journey toward an expected end uniquely suited to your design and calling.

As you move forward from these pages, remember that the Master who touched my life touches yours as well. The purpose He has for you may not look like anyone else's. The path He leads you on may not follow conventional routes to success. The contribution He calls you to make may not fit traditional categories or expectations.

But it will be exactly right for who you are, for how you're designed, for what the world needs from you specifically. It will be your expected end—the purpose for which you were created, the contribution only you can make, the life only you can live.

You can do it.

PERSONAL REFLECTION

Jeremiah 29:11 promises an "expected end" — a divine purpose that gives meaning to our journey, even when that journey includes unexpected challenges, detours, and difficulties. For much of my life, I misunderstood what this meant. I thought the "expected end" would be overcoming my limitations to become like everyone else — reading fluently, writing easily, processing information quickly, succeeding by conventional standards.

But God's "expected end" for me wasn't about becoming someone else; it was about becoming fully myself — the unique person He designed me to be, with specific purposes only I could fulfill. It wasn't about eliminating my differences but about revealing their purpose. It wasn't about conforming to others' expectations but about discovering and embracing divine intention.

I now understand that being born stillborn, struggling with learning, being diagnosed with ADHD at 37 — all of it was part of the journey toward this "expected end." None of it was wasted. None of it was a mistake. None of it was punishment. All of it was preparation for ministry that someone with a different journey couldn't offer, for connections with people others might not reach, for perspectives on scripture and life others might not provide.

This doesn't mean God causes suffering or creates disabilities. But it does mean that in His redemptive love, He weaves even our challenges into the tapestry of purpose, using what others might discard or dismiss as essential threads in the design. The "expected end" isn't the absence of difficulty; it's the presence of meaning and purpose that transcends it.

Whatever journey you're on — with whatever challenges, limitations, or differences you face— know that it leads to an "expected end" uniquely suited to your design and calling. Not because every difficulty is divinely ordained, but because the Master's touch can transform every experience — even painful ones — into preparation for purpose only you can fulfill.

REFLECTION QUESTIONS

1. How has your perspective on your own challenges or limitations changed through reading this book?

2. In what ways might your unique journey be preparing you for contributions only you can make?

3. Which of the five steps—Accept Your Difference, Seek Help, Stop Comparing, Surround Yourself with Supporters, Forgive and Be Grateful— do you most need to focus on right now?

4. How might your own challenges qualify you to offer unique understanding or assistance to others facing similar journeys?

5. What would embracing your "expected end" look like in your life today—not someday in the future, but in your current circumstances and relationships?

APPENDIX: RESOURCES FOR YOUR JOURNEY

Throughout this book, I've shared my personal journey with ADHD and learning differences. While my path has been shaped by faith and divine purpose, I recognize that practical resources can be invaluable companions on the journey. This appendix provides information that might be helpful as you navigate your own path or support someone else on theirs.

UNDERSTANDING ADHD

Organizations and Websites

CHADD (Children and Adults with Attention-Deficit/Hyperactivity Disorder)
Website: www.chadd.org
A leading resource for information, training, and advocacy for ADHD. They offer support groups, webinars, conferences, and a helpline.

Attention Deficit Disorder Association (ADDA)
Website: www.add.org

Focused specifically on adults with ADHD, providing resources, support, and community.

ADDitude Magazine
Website: www.additudemag.com
Offers articles, webinars, and resources about living with ADHD, with sections for parents, adults, and educators.

Understood
Website: www.understood.org

Provides resources for learning and thinking differences, including ADHD, dyslexia, and other challenges.

Books on ADHD

"Driven to Distraction" by Edward M. Hallowell, MD and John J. Ratey, MD A comprehensive guide to understanding and living with ADHD, written by experts who both have ADHD themselves.

"Taking Charge of Adult ADHD" by Russell A. Barkley, PhD

Practical strategies for adults with ADHD, based on scientific research.

"You Mean I'm Not Lazy, Stupid or Crazy?!" by Kate Kelly and Peggy Ramundo
A self-help book for adults with ADHD, written by authors who have ADHD.

"The ADHD Effect on Marriage" by Melissa Orlov
Explores how ADHD can affect relationships and offers strategies for strengthening marriages affected by ADHD.

FAITH-BASED RESOURCES

Books

"Different: The Story of an Outside-the-Box Kid and the Mom Who Loved Him" by Sally Clarkson and Nathan Clarkson
A mother and son's journey with learning differences and mental health challenges, from a faith perspective.

"Gifted Minds: Empowering Your Child with Learning Differences" by Dr. Kathy Koch
Explores how to nurture the gifts within children who learn differently.

"God's Word on Mental Health: 60 Devotional Readings" by Stephen Arterburn and Becky Johnson
Devotional readings that apply biblical principles to mental health challenges.

Ministries and Organizations

Key Ministry
Website: www.keyministry.org
Provides resources to help churches welcome and include families affected by disabilities, including mental health conditions.

Joni and Friends
Website: www.joniandfriends.org
Christian organization focused on disability ministry and resources.

Mental Health Grace Alliance
Website: www.mentalhealthgracealliance.org
Faith-based support for mental health challenges, including support groups and resources.

EDUCATIONAL RESOURCES

Learning Accommodations

National Center for Learning Disabilities
Website: www.ncld.org
Provides information about accommodations, legal rights, and advocacy for individuals with learning differences.

Learning Disabilities Association of America
Website: www.ldaamerica.org
Offers resources for understanding various learning disabilities and strategies for success.

Alternative Learning Methods

Visual Learning Resources

- Khan Academy (www.khanacademy.org): Free video-based learning on numerous subjects
- YouTube Educational Channels: Crash Course, TED-Ed, SciShow
- Mind mapping tools: MindMeister, XMind, Coggle

Audiobooks and Text-to-Speech Technology

- Learning Ally: www.learningally.org
- Bookshare: www.bookshare.org
- Audible: www.audible.com
- Natural Reader: www.naturalreaders.com

Speech-to-Text Tools

- Dragon Naturally Speaking
- Google Docs Voice Typing
- Apple Dictation
- Microsoft Dictate

THERAPEUTIC RESOURCES

Finding a Therapist

Psychology Today Therapist Finder
 Website: www.psychologytoday.com/us/therapists
Search for therapists by specialty, insurance, location, and more.

American Psychological Association Psychologist Locator

Website: locator.apa.org Find psychologists in your area.

SAMHSA Treatment Locator
 Website: www.findtreatment.samhsa.gov
Helpline: 1-800-662-HELP (4357)
Find mental health and substance use treatment facilities.

Types of Therapy That May Help ADHD

Cognitive Behavioral Therapy (CBT)
Helps develop skills for managing thoughts, behaviors, and emotions.

ADHD Coaching
Works on practical strategies for organization, time management, and goal setting.

Mindfulness-Based Interventions
Practices that can improve attention, reduce stress, and increase selfawareness.

WORKPLACE RESOURCES

Job Accommodations Network (JAN)

Website: askjan.org
Information about workplace accommodations and disability employment issues.

Americans with Disabilities Act (ADA) Information

Website: www.ada.gov
Information about rights and responsibilities under the ADA.

Workplace Strategies for Adults with ADHD
- Time management tools: Pomodoro Technique, Time Timer
- Organization apps: Trello, Asana, Todoist
- Focus apps: Forest, Freedom, Focus@Will

A PERSONAL NOTE

Remember that no resource can replace the power of personal connection and community. As I've shared throughout this book, relationships have been central to my journey. Seek out supportive individuals, groups, or communities—whether in person or online—who understand your challenges and believe in your potential.

Also remember that what works for one person may not work for another. ADHD and learning differences manifest uniquely in each individual. Be patient with yourself as you discover which strategies, tools, and resources work best for you.

Most importantly, keep in mind that your differences are part of your unique design. They present challenges, yes, but they also equip you for contributions only you can make. The Master's touch is evident not just in those who fit conventional molds but in every unique individual willing to embrace their design and purpose.

You can do it.

— Kenneth R. Gillard

SCRIPTURE BIBLIOGRAPHY

Throughout my journey, certain passages of scripture have been anchors for my soul, lighthouses in the darkness, and foundations for my understanding of God's purpose in my life. These verses weren't just inspirational quotes; they were divine declarations that shaped my identity and calling. I share them here as a resource for your own journey.

IDENTITY AND PURPOSE

Jeremiah 1:4-5
"Then the word of the LORD came unto me, saying, Before I formed thee in the belly I knew thee; and before thou camest forth out of the womb I sanctified thee, and I ordained thee a prophet unto the nations."

This scripture transformed how I viewed my birth as a premature, stillborn baby who wasn't breathing. It wasn't random; it was part of God's intentional design. He knew me before I was formed. He had purposes for me before I took my first breath. This verse helped me see that my learning differences weren't mistakes but part of His plan for my life and ministry.

Psalm 139:14
"I will praise thee; for I am fearfully and wonderfully made: marvellous are thy works; and that my soul knoweth right well."

When I discovered I had ADHD at age 37, this verse took on new meaning. I wasn't defective; I was "fearfully and wonderfully made" exactly as God intended. My brain worked differently not because of divine oversight but because of divine design. This scripture helped me accept and eventually celebrate my unique wiring rather than fighting against it.

Jeremiah 29:11
"For I know the thoughts that I think toward you, saith the LORD, thoughts of peace, and not of evil, to give you an expected end."

This verse assured me that God had good intentions for my life, even when circumstances suggested otherwise. The "expected end" wasn't about becoming like everyone else but becoming exactly who He designed me to be. This scripture helped me trust divine purpose even when the path wasn't clear or conventional.

STRENGTH AND COURAGE

Philippians 4:13
"I can do all things through Christ which strengtheneth me."

This became my mantra when facing challenges that seemed insurmountable. It wasn't about my abilities but about Christ's strength working through me. It wasn't a guarantee that everything would be easy but a promise that I wouldn't face anything alone. My mother's constant encouragement — "You can do it, Kenny" — echoed this spiritual truth.

Romans 8:31
"What shall we then say to these things? If God be for us, who can be against us?"

God gave me this scripture on my 31st birthday (February 8, 1993). It became particularly meaningful as I faced opposition or doubt from others. It reminded me that God's opinion of me mattered more than human judgments, that His purposes for me would prevail despite obstacles.

2 Corinthians 5:7
"For we walk by faith, not by sight."

Living with ADHD taught me a profound interpretation of this verse. Walking by faith means trusting God's design when society sees only disorder. It means believing in divine purpose when educational systems see only deficiency. It means recognizing the Master's touch even when others see only limitation.

DIVINE PERSPECTIVE

Romans 8:28
"And we know that all things work together for good to them that love God, to them who are the called according to his purpose."

When I struggled to understand why certain doors closed or why particular challenges persisted, this verse provided perspective. It assured me that nothing was wasted, that every experience — even painful ones — was being woven into a larger purpose. This didn't make difficulties easy, but it made them meaningful.

1 Samuel 16:7
"But the LORD said unto Samuel, Look not on his countenance, or on the height of his stature; because I have refused him: for the LORD seeth not as man seeth; for man looketh on the outward appearance, but the LORD looketh on the heart."

This scripture shaped how I approached jail ministry. When others saw inmates defined by their crimes or their orange jumpsuits, I tried to see as God sees— looking beyond external circumstances to the heart within. Having experienced being labeled and limited, I could recognize that pain in others and respond with God's perspective rather than human judgment.

Proverbs 22:6

"Train up a child in the way he should go: and when he is old, he will not depart from it."

I came to understand this verse not as training all children the same way, but as training each child according to their unique design. My mother and the community around me didn't try to force me into a standard mold. They recognized my visual learning style and trained me accordingly. This deeper wisdom has shaped how I mentor others.

COMMUNITY AND RELATIONSHIPS

Proverbs 27:17
"Iron sharpeneth iron; so a man sharpeneth the countenance of his friend."

This verse captures the transformative power of authentic relationships. Through connections with mentors, therapists, peers, and those I mentored, I experienced mutual growth and refinement. Iron sharpening iron isn't a one-way process— both pieces are affected, both become sharper, both are transformed by the friction.

Colossians 3:23
"And whatsoever ye do, do it heartily, as to the Lord, and not unto men."

Working "heartily" means bringing your whole self—your unique design, your particular gifts, your distinct perspective—to whatever work God places before you. This verse transformed how I viewed even seemingly ordinary tasks, from driving the bus to cleaning the church as a janitor. It gave spiritual significance to practical service.

1 John 4:4

"Ye are of God, little children, and have overcome them: because greater is he that is in you, than he that is in the world."

When I faced discouragement or doubt about my abilities, this verse reminded me that the power within me—God's Spirit—was greater than any obstacle or limitation I faced. It wasn't about my capabilities but about God working through me, using even my differences for His purposes.

COMFORT AND HEALING

Psalm 34:18

"The LORD is nigh unto them that are of a broken heart; and saveth such as be of a contrite spirit."

During times of depression, when the weight of labels and limitations felt overwhelming, this verse assured me of God's presence in my pain. He wasn't distant from my struggles; He was especially near in them. This brought comfort when I felt most alone or misunderstood.

Isaiah 40:31

"But they that wait upon the LORD shall renew their strength; they shall mount up with wings as eagles; they shall run, and not be weary; and they shall walk, and not faint."

The journey with ADHD and learning differences requires patience—with yourself and with processes that might take longer than conventional paths. This verse encouraged me during waiting seasons, reminding me that divine timing often differs from human expectations, and that strength comes through trust and perseverance.

Matthew 25:36
"I was in prison, and ye came unto me."

This verse took on deeper meaning through my jail ministry. I realized Jesus wasn't just speaking about our ministry to prisoners but about His presence with them —and with us — in places of confinement, whether physical prisons or the mental, emotional, and spiritual prisons that confine so many of us.

These scriptures aren't just verses to memorize; they're truths to internalize and live by. They continue to shape my understanding of God's purpose for my life, His perspective on my challenges, and His presence through every step of the journey. May they bring similar illumination and comfort to you, whatever path you're walking.

— Kenneth R. Gillard

ACKNOWLEDGMENTS

I would like to share my heartfelt gratitude to the many people who have shaped my life and helped me become the man I am today. Their influence, guidance, and support have been manifestations of the Master's touch working through human hands.

Community Family

I acknowledge the contributions of these souls in my community who have made the transition from labor to reward:

From Howard Street: I thank Mr. and Mrs. James and Lois Nichols, Deacon
Nolan and Lena Adams, Mr. and Mrs. James and Edith Wilson, Mother Tinnie
Smith, Mr. and Mrs. Earl and Lillian Funderburk, Mrs. Mary Kennedy, Elder Arthur
Adams, Mr. and Mrs. Bob and Jewel Silk and family, Mr. and Mrs. Henry and Anne Fielder, Mr. and Mrs. Verree and Laura Henderson.

From the Southside Community: Mr. and Mrs. Eugene Clark, Mr. and Mrs. Robert and Alvester Anderson, Aunt Hattie Campbell, Mary Henry, Pastor Donald and Wonda Alston, Etta Copedge and family, Sister Patricia Harden Harasim and Mrs. Quarles.

Church Family

Also in the next world: I am grateful to my Mount Olive Family: The Pastor
R.R. and Annie Turpin, Pastor Roy I. Greer III and Lois Greer, Pastor Major and the late First Lady Stewart and Family, The Rev. Simon Barbee, Alice Barbee, Mother Pauline Todd and family, Mrs. Ann Thompson and family, Mrs. Queen Matthews, Mrs. Mary Wynn and her late daughter Della Wynn, Deacon Wilbur and the late Mildred Payne and family, Brother Bill and Sister Dorothy Pennix and family, Mrs. Dorothy Hickman, Richard Battle, Howard Keels, and the Mount Olive Baptist Church congregation who nurtured me from childhood. My thanks also to Quinn Chapel AME Church and the late Pastor Braxton Burgess and the entire congregation, Dad and Mother Flippen and family.

And these are still serving the Body of Christ:

Sister Doris Smiley, Brother Bob Patterson, Mother Jimmie Maxwell, Auntie Anne McCloud, Deacon Clyde and Corine Edwards, Mother Dorthy Laws, Mother Edith Spencer, Mrs. Claudette Kennedy and family, Sister Jackie Hill, Sister A Lavalley and family, Thelma Byers and daughter Saryne Byers and family, `and Mrs. Corrine Adams.

To The Heart Church in Grand Rapids, Michigan: Pastor George and First Lady Davis and the entire congregation — thank you for welcoming me during a period of transition.

I am grateful to the New Jerusalem Full Gospel Baptist Church, the late Pastor Patrick Sanders, First Lady Sanders and their family, Mother Mary Williams and family, Deacon Daniel Hall and Mother Hall, and the entire church family. All these souls provided a spiritual home when I needed it most.

I acknowledge with gratitude the former Hill Road Baptist Church in Grand Blanc, Michigan, where I served as pastor and experienced growth and purpose.

Mentors and Friends

My life has been enriched by numerous mentors and teachers:
the YMCA, Big Brothers, Junior Achievement, The late Pastor Roosevelt and the late First Lady N. Austin, The late Deacon Samuel Wilson, The late Brother JT Williams, the late Mrs. Sybil Blount, the late Mrs. Naomi Dilworth and family, the late Mr. and Mrs. Fred Jordan and family, the late Mother Louise Jackson and the entire Jackson family, the late Brother William Tipper and family, the late Bessie Hill Evans and her late daughter Altha Evans, and the late Marcia Blount.

To my friends of mention:
Greg Henry, Paul Gage, Ron Hughes, Charles Henry, Pastor Keith Ireland, Rev.
Torrey Walthour, Betty Tipper and family, Pastor Charles Dantzler and family, and
Rev. Cary D. Brassfield and entire family. Ivan Griffin and Dr Michael Brocree,
Frank Lane and wife Bonnie Lane, Keith Bradford and Derrick Thompson, Clayton Pirtle and family, Dr. David and Melody Wiese and family, Lyle Reynolds, John Caruth and family.

Special thanks to:

My special sister Mrs. Lee Ella Gillard Ross, Galilean Baptist Church, Pastor Sean Payne, First Lady Sonya Payne, Mr. Darren James McConkey and entire family, Dr. J Fredrick Bland, Dr. Chris Shreve, Marta Konrad, Sheriff Chris Swanson and the Genesee County Jail, and Dr. Ruben West and family.

My Spiritual Sons:
Pastor Mike Garrison, Minister Brad Robinson, George Huddleston, Baridi Hasan, JT Tiner, and many others. You know who you are.

My Spiritual Brothers:
Pastor Keith Ireland, Pastor Sean Payne, Antoine Walker, Shaphan Abron, The late Pastor Marnell Wright, and Jamil Cooper Jr. Pastor Alfred Harris Sr., Pastor Frank Gilliard, Pastor Paul Todd, Pastor Emil Thomas, Mark Payne, Reverend David Greer and Reverend Michael Greer, and many others.

My Spiritual Sisters:
Wildean Payne, Tonya Battle, Janet Poole Little, Marnice Roberts, Monica
Huddleston, Lisa Payton, Sheryl Payton, Lurenda Shelby, Gloria Dukes, Diane Williams, Brenda Gordon, Pat Hennie, The Barbee Sisters, The Wynn Sisters, Angela Feaster and many many more.

Sisters: thank you for being in my life.

There are countless others I could name — all these people have poured into my life in ways I cannot fully express. They are just a few of the many who have contributed to my journey.

A Message of Encouragement

The Master's touch has been evident in my life through these relationships. The Master touched their hearts, and in turn, they touched mine, bringing me to where I am today.

I want to encourage you that there are people waiting for you, people who are cheering for you, people who believe in you. You can do it. You can move from where you are to where you're meant to be, but you must look deep within yourself and surround yourself with good people — people who speak well into your life and encourage you. These may not always speak the way you want them to speak about you, but they are honest, truthful, loving, and believe the best for you and your life.

You must continue to move forward each day, regardless of the challenges you face or those that lie ahead. Move forward with hope, vigor, fortitude, courage, integrity, character, endurance, and even through suffering. These qualities shape you, and though at times it may appear you're being broken, I guarantee you're being made better.

We were not placed on this earth to be alone. We were created to build relationships with one another — to connect, love, build up, and encourage one another. These connections will sustain anyone going through life's challenges.

If you have this kind of support surrounding you, you have a tremendous advantage, and I encourage you to continue nurturing these relationships throughout your life. Many of the people I've named have passed on to be with the Lord, but the love, wisdom, knowledge, and experiences they shared with me continue to influence who I am today.

With deep gratitude,
Kenneth R. Gillard

About the Author

Kenneth R. Gillard

Kenneth R. Gillard is not a writer by profession, but a remarkable individual whose profound insights and life experiences form the heart of *The Master's Touch*. This book emerges from Kenneth's personal journals — a collection of oratory notes that capture his unique ability to understand and articulate the deep principles of mentorship, skill, and human potential.

Throughout his life, Pastor Gillard has been a master of human connection, possessing an extraordinary gift for understanding the intricate dynamics of learning, growth, and personal transformation. His journals reflect decades of observations, conversations, and reflections gathered from his rich and diverse experiences across various walks of life.

The Master's Touch is not a traditional authored book, but a carefully curated compilation of Kenneth's most profound thoughts and insights. Edited by Boyd Michaels, the book brings to light the raw, unfiltered wisdom that Kenneth has accumulated through his lifetime of learning and teaching.

Known for his ability to connect with people on a deeply meaningful level, Kenneth Gillard has been a mentor, a listener, and a storyteller in the truest sense. His life's work has been about understanding the subtle art of knowledge transmission —how skills, wisdom, and human potential are shared across generations.

This book stands as a testament to Kenneth's remarkable journey — a collection of insights that go far beyond traditional writing, offering readers a window into a lifetime of deep understanding and human connection.

www.ingramcontent.com/pod-product-compliance
Lightning Source LLC
Chambersburg PA
CBHW050328010526
44119CB00050B/715